"The Institute of HeartMath is a leader in developing innovative techniques to harmonize body and mind. The Cut-Thru method is based on solid science, and will add joy and fulfillment to the lives of those who use it."

Larry Dossey, M.D.,
author of *Healing Words* and *Recovering the Soul*

"There is no way to praise Cut-Thru sufficiently, nor can its potential for bringing dramatic change to the individual and to society be overstated. As with Childre's other works, here is genius expressed with exquisite simplicity and eminently practical steps for application to daily life. His new observations on bringing heart and mind into synchrony may well be the most important offerings of our times."

Joseph Chilton Pearce,
author of *Evolution's End* and *Crack in the Cosmic Egg*

Other Books and Music by DOC LEW CHILDRE

*Self Empowerment:
The Heart Approach to Stress Management*

*FREEZE-FRAME:
Fast Action Stress Relief;
A Scientifically Proven Technique*

FREEZE-FRAME Audiobook

CUT-THRU Audiobook

The How To Book of Teen Self Discovery

*A Parenting Manual:
Heart Hope For the Family*

*Teaching Children To Love:
55 Games and Fun Activities for
Raising Balanced Children in Unbalanced Times*

*Women Lead With Their Hearts:
The New Paradigm and New Solution for the 21st Century
— A White Paper —*

Heart Zones (cassette and CD)

Speed of Balance (cassette and CD)

CUT-THRU®

Achieve Total Security and Maximum Energy

A Scientifically Proven Insight
on How To *Care*
Without Becoming a Victim

by
Doc Lew Childre

Edited by Deborah Rozman, Ph.D.

PLANETARY PUBLICATIONS
Boulder Creek, California

4

CUT-THRU is a registered trademark of the Institute of HeartMath.

Published in the United States of America by:

Planetary Publications

P.O. Box 66, Boulder Creek, California 95006

(800) 372-3100   (408) 338-2161   Fax (408) 338-9861

hrtmath@netcom.com

http://www.webcom.com/hrtmath

Manufactured in the United States of America by BookCrafters

First Printing 1995

Cover Design by Sandy Royall

Library of Congress Cataloging in Publication Data

Childre, Doc Lew, 1945-

Cut-Thru: achieve total security and maximum energy; a scientifically proven insight on how to care without becoming a victim / by Doc Lew Childre; edited by Dobrah Rozman.

p. cm.

Includes bibliographical references.

ISBN 1-879052-33-4

1. Emotional maturity. 2. Problem solving. 3. Quality of life—Psychological aspects. I. Rozman, Deborah II. Title.

BF710.C 48 1996

158--dc20   95-26111

CIP

10 9 8 7 6 5 4 3 2 1

Table of Contents

Author's Preface

E motional stress has become a global virus, infecting families, schools, businesses, governments, as well as individuals. Because of the tremendous need for practical solutions to the emotional stress momentum, I researched and developed CUT-THRU®. In today's society, people are trying to cope with rapid change but many feel disempowered and drained. CUT-THRU is a power tool to take you beyond coping into empowered management. As the speed of change continues to accelerate, many will look for power tools to increase their happiness, security, and sense of personal control. It's easy to feel victimized when you feel you have little control over what's happening around you. But people have the power to change the one thing they do have control over — themselves. They just need to know how.

The CUT-THRU book is in part a report on the scientific findings at the Institute of HeartMath (IHM), a nonprofit research and training organization in Boulder Creek, California. Incorporated in 1991, IHM is dedicated to providing stress solutions and innovative approaches to quality, creativity, and intuitive development. IHM laboratories specialize in both the electrophysiology of the human system and psychoneuroimmunology. Our scientific papers have been published in prominent medical journals, including the *American Journal of Cardiology.*

Following twenty years of focused research on the brain, mind, and heart, I founded IHM with the mission of putting the heart back into the people business. One of the key findings of IHM scientists is that the heart isn't just a physical pump nor a metaphorical symbol for feeling. The heart is a center for intelligence within the human system. As the famous 17th century French mathematician and physicist Pascal said, *"The heart has reasons that reason knows not of."* When people learn to listen to their heart, they find a source of strength, power, and intuitive intelligence. IHM's self-management tools teach people how to go deep in the heart to find solutions to problems, enhance emotional well-being, and advance intelligent understanding. Our training programs have been acclaimed by individuals and companies throughout the world. The testing and development of the CUT-THRU technology took place over several years. Until now, the tool was only taught to those participating in research or attending selected seminars at IHM. Now, after years of experience, testing, and refinement, CUT-THRU is offered in this book.

Most people have never been educated on how to release disturbed feelings and thoughts. Instead, they vent, analyze, or repress them in order to get rid of them. Yet, the stress still accumulates. Emotions and perceptions affect our hormones, which in turn affect our emotions and perceptions in a continuous cycle. For many, stress problems have become so intricate and entwined that they seem unresolvable. CUT-THRU shows people how to increase their intelligence and self-correct distortions in emotions, perceptions, and their biological consequences. It empowers people to become their own self-pharmacists, balancing their internal hormonal prescriptions and recouping energy and time lost from emotional and mental stress.

Increased intelligence means not having to repeat the same old stresses. In Greek mythology, Gordius, king of Phrygia, tied a knot so entwined that no one could untie it. According to the legend, whoever could untie the knot would become ruler of all Asia. Alexander the Great, seeing that the knot could not be untied, *cut thru* it with his sword and became the ruler. The CUT-THRU technique shows people how "to cut thru the gordian knot" of emotional stress. Of course, this doesn't mean that everyone needs stress relief. If you already are happy, secure, and energetic, CUT-THRU can take you to new levels of self-management and empowerment to increase your potential talents. It can strengthen your regenerative and creative capacities. When emotions are in balance and aligned with your real heart, you free a tremendous amount of energy to expand talents and creativity. Bringing the emotions in phase with the heart generates a *time shift* in personal effectiveness. This results in preventive maintenance — preventing unnecessary dips in energy, loss of time, and having to recoup.

Doctors prescribe regimens for patients, knowing that if patients would just follow instructions, their problems would most likely improve. The doctor is offering patients a time shift out of their problems — accelerating the healing process — but many don't take it. They practice or do a little and come back to the doctor again and again. Their problems continue when they could have been resolved — and that's a time and energy loss. Every time you sincerely use CUT-THRU, you activate the power to create a time shift into a new level of energy and insight. Test the tool for yourself. If there is an attitude you need to change or an aspect of your life that you want to improve, CUT-THRU can help. It shows you how to time shift, instead of just coping or trying to work something out.

Many people want more inner peace, quality, fun, and adventure. But they have to CUT-THRU the insecurities and energy drains that short circuit fulfillment. Those who compete in marathons learn to self-manage their physical bodies at a refined level, but they can still be hostile, depressed, insecure, and fatigued if they can't manage their emotions. Cut-Thru prevents emotions from engulfing you and dragging you through the drain process. Based on scientific investigation of the heart-brain communication system (the inner information highway), Cut-Thru shows you how to find real peace and harmony on all levels — mental, emotional, and physical.

The lack of emotional management is a planetary ailment. Emotional stress is a major predator of peace in individuals, the environment, the home, and the whole of society. The intentions of this book are aimed at the facilitation of this global problem. But people have to first become aware of the problem, then remedy it. As you read, listen to your own heart for insights on where you can use the tool, then act on your insights. I respect that people have different ways for arriving at the same goal; nevertheless Cut-Thru is a method that works. As you listen to and follow your heart intelligence, you'll find new security, freedom, and vitality.

Doc Lew Childre
Boulder Creek, California

Chapter 1

What's Happened to Care?

The world is experiencing an unprecedented degree of change. Change is widespread and accelerating, occurring within the family, the workplace, political structures, and within oneself. Technological advances have linked the globe in a world wide information network. People are increasingly stressed, and the emotional quality of life has deteriorated for many.

The confusion and chaos occurring in society is largely due to forgetting or ignoring the heart. As we transition through rapid change, it's essential to bring the heart and care into the decision-making process. The mind alone won't cut it. From a global perspective, the relentless focus on educating the brain/mind has not solved our personal or social problems. In fact, many problems are getting worse — anxiety, depression, addiction, crime, violence, homelessness, etc. It's time for a shift from a focus on mind alone to an inclusion of heart and feeling. The feeling quality of life has eluded modern thinkers. The assumption has been that rational thought alone can direct feelings in ways that are beneficial for oneself and the whole.

So we keep looking to technology for answers. We search for the causes of human behavior in genetic codes with the hope that this will give us direction in how to improve behavior. We look to the brain for the cause of aberrant emotions with the hope of finding drugs to cure emotional problems. In scientific methodology, we try to eliminate feeling from the analytical process so we can remain "objective." The brain can block out the heart from our lives but often with disastrous consequences. When we learn to think with the heart, engaging the brain/mind in teamwork with the heart, we teach ourselves to operate in more intelligent and productive ways.

It's no coincidence that business leaders are starting to talk about the importance of leading with the heart. Three years ago that type of discussion would have appeared soft, impractical, unproductive. Today, the feelings of the heart are becoming recognized as an aspect of intelligence that cannot be disregarded and could be the key to the future of our organizations, our families, and the human race itself. The heart is crucial for health and emotional balance in life. It is also crucial for achieving personal, family, business, and social goals. While this view of the heart has long been ignored by researchers, many are rethinking this ignorance. It's time to understand the heart and the enormous role that it plays in decision-making and overall quality of life.

People are often told, "Don't just react, put your thinking cap on," or "Use your mind, not your heart." The assumption is that emotions will color your common sense and lead you astray. However, people are also told, "Follow your heart," to find your deeper values or actualize your goals. It appears to be a paradox until we gain a more advanced understanding.

There are several domains of intelligence within the human system, including mental intelligence, emotional intelligence, and cellular intelligence, each of which can act independently. It's within the intuitive domain that I call *heart intelligence* where we find the harmonious integration of all other aspects of intelligence. What I'm suggesting is that *the physical heart* is the central distribution station from which intuitive regulation is offered for the benefit of one's mental, emotional, and physical systems.

Heart intelligence entrains (synchronizes) the emotions and mind, increasing both emotional and mental intelligence, bringing them into coherence and harmony. This entrainment is communicated to the cellular intelligence that regulates our unconscious body functions. It's the balance and entrainment of our entire system that results in increased health and extra energy. The practice of following your heart intelligence will bring all your systems into the balanced internal state called "flow." Mihaly Csikszentmihalyi, author of *Flow: The Psychology of Optimal Experience*, defines "flow" as a state of joy, creativity, the process of total involvement with life where we feel in control of our actions and a deep sense of enjoyment. He goes on to state that, *"Flow* is the way people describe their state of mind when consciousness is harmoniously ordered."[1] This stops payment on unhappiness and life becomes enriched.

Without heart intelligence, the untamed mind and emotions drain your energies and keep you duped into believing that your vitality is being squandered. It's from heart intelligence that you gain the insight and power to care for yourself and make attitude adjustments that reduce stress and recoup energy spent from repetitive stress encounters. The heart is a major entry point for more of your own spirit to manifest, allowing you to become more of your *real self.* When acting from your heart intelligence, your decisions, your goal planning, your communications, and your actions benefit yourself and everyone.

Inner Technology

Technology is the application of knowledge for practical ends, an invention, process, or method. The application of knowledge for the practical end of improving our emotional quality of life must address the *inner quality* of our feelings and thoughts. In fact, without inner quality, the externals don't seem to matter after a certain point.

This book will explore new inner technology that can bring dynamic vitality and security to the world in which we spend all our waking hours — the world of our feelings and thoughts. This is where we create misery or satisfaction. CUT-THRU provides a method for entraining heart, mind, and body that yields balance and coherence. What is *coherence*? Strictly speaking, coherence is the act or state of cohering, cohesion, congruity; logically connected; having a natural agreement of parts; harmonious.

When we are coherent, we feel good, think clearly, and make quality decisions. When we are incoherent, we feel anxious, confused, and our decision-making process is impaired. A lack of coherence perpetuates misguided thinking, upside-down perspectives such as putting money before family, and ongoing disappointments, divorces, poor health, famines, wars, misery. Lack of emotional coherence undermines people's best efforts and constructs the "road to hell that's paved with good intentions."

The key to coherence lies within the heart — both the physical heart and the feelings associated with heart. That's where the central intelligence of your real spirit is sourced. CUT-THRU is a scientifically validated methodology to access this heart intelligence. It starts with energizing basic *core heart values* of love, care, compassion, and appreciation. It's important to understand that these are not only values, but feelings. Feelings that are powerful. In new breakthrough research, love, care, compassion, and appreciation have been shown in the laboratory to generate increased coherence in the heart's electrical system which is then communicated to the brain and to every cell of the body.[2] These positive feelings affect how we perceive and respond to life. They affect health and aging. They affect our ability to care for ourselves and others. When our relationships or our workplaces lack these core heart feelings, stress is the inevitable result.

Babies are born with natural expressions of love, care, compassion, and appreciation. Parents try to cultivate these qualities in their children. So why do these qualities become so sparse in family and social interactions that we are left with over a 50% divorce rate, children who are killing each other, and raging violence? Why does the world seem like such an uncaring place, even though people are trying to care for families, friends, jobs, and society? Caring doesn't seem to be enough. Most of us were taught that "to care" is supposed to bring joy and happiness. Instead, men and women complain of how stressed, tired, and worn out they are from always caring. Have we cared too much?

What is Care?

Webster's dictionary defines "care" first and foremost as a source of anxiety: "a troubled or burdened state of mind; worry; concern."[3] Certainly, this describes the state of today's world — quite different from the heartwarming feelings of care that people look for and value. A few definitions later, Webster's goes on to state that "care" is also "to feel love for, to look after, provide for, attend to." How is it that a longing to love, care for, or protect, becomes such a troubling burden?

In examining my own life a number of years ago, I realized that in caring for people, I would frequently worry about them, wonder if they were okay, and get upset if their problems kept growing in spite of my efforts to help them. I became anxious and concerned. Why? "Because I care," I told myself. Yet, it puzzled me that my caring efforts kept draining me. I felt I was carrying the world on my back and wondered, "Is it worth it?"

In studying this enigma, it became obvious to me that I was caring too much about non-essentials. And on important matters, I was taking care *over a line and into stress*. I realized I wasn't alone. That's what most people do. I decided to research this type of stress-producing care and coined it "overcare." Overcare is care that becomes a drain or deficit in the human system, offering no sight of any real solution to a problem. It takes you out of "flow." When you overcare about what you love, care about, feel compassion for, or appreciate, the stress that is produced generates *incoherent* frequencies in the electrical system of the heart, and that incoherence is communicated to the brain and every cell in the body.[2] When people keep worrying about the things they care about, they dig themselves into a pit of endless anxiety. Overcare always spawns stress. The world has become stagnant from overcare and the result is a widespread feeling of "no hope."

Stress and Overcare Statistics and Examples

What is stress? Stress is often viewed as a mental, emotional, or physiological response, such as tension, resistance, worry, strain, frustration, etc., that interferes with normal physiological and psychological equilibrium. If psychological equilibrium is disturbed for too long, the stress becomes disabling. That's when we feel we are out of control or can't get a grip on life. At the 1995 International Congress on Stress, Dr. Graham Burrows announced that, after reviewing thousands of studies on stress, the problem of stress could be reduced to two basic causes: problems in perception and problems in communication. At the Institute of HeartMath (IHM), we define stress as *"an inharmonious energy or experience that results from our inefficient mental or emotional perceptions and responses to people, places, issues, or events in life."* Because stress is a *response* — not the event that triggers the response — it changes as our perceptions change. Once we broaden our perception of a situation, the stressful reaction is released. Therefore, at IHM, researchers also define stress as *an untransformed opportunity for empowerment.*

The Mitchum Report on Stress in the '90s displayed that for most people work and money are continuous sources of worry, anxiety, and stress.[4] In the U.S., 58% of those surveyed said they worry most about work-related issues and 51% worry about money. For 25% of Americans, conflict between work and family is a frequent source of lack of equilibrium, tension, and stress. This survey also divulged two new major stressors that have surfaced: 51% worry about time for self and 33% worry about the environment. Many small incidents also cause stress: when late for an appointment 59% report feeling stressed, 55% find paying bills stressful, and 57% are stressed when they have to wait in traffic or stand in line at a store. These small daily stresses stack up. Add to that stack a serious stress regarding money, job, family, someone close who is seriously ill or dying, and it's easy to see why people are so stressed out they have no energy left to keep on caring.

Stress Accumulators

What the statistics indicate is that people are trying to care, but *overcare* is re-energizing their worry and perpetuating their stress. True care, on the other hand, brings inner coherence. Genuine care tenders life for the purpose of joy and understanding. When genuine care turns to a depletion of energy and stressing over what you care about, recognize that *it's the result of overcare*. Overcare is when you start in the right direction but somehow end up at a dead end. Eventually, there is no motivation or energy left and it's easier just to quit caring.

Overcare is often most obvious in relationships. When someone doesn't respond to your care in the way you had hoped, worry sets in. The genuine caring feeling fades under anxious self-questioning: "Is she okay?" "Did I do something to offend?" Insecurities abound when overcare takes hold. From this deficit position, people try everything they can think of to help the situation, but find themselves at a loss not knowing what to do. Consider Sam, who cared about his job but had a difficult boss. He did everything he knew to please the boss, but was constantly criticized. He worried about whether he would ever succeed, so he worked longer hours at the expense of his wife, family, and personal needs. He was extremely stressed. At the end of the year, when he was not given a long-awaited promotion, he found himself too worn out to care anymore. Millions of people can relate to this scenario.

Burnout

The nursing profession has one of the highest rates of stress and burnout. In a study on caregiving among nurses, researcher Carol L. Montgomery, R.N., Ph.D., reports: "Caregivers have always lived with the paradox that they are supposed to care deeply about their clients, but not get too involved. In addition, caring itself has been viewed as dangerous for the one caring, such that caregivers are urged not to care too much, for fear of burnout (Maslach, 1983)." The study endeavored to determine the nature of caring communication, and what this experience is for the caregiver.[5] Is it associated with burnout, or is caring the essence of professional satisfaction? Dr. Montgomery asked, "If both situations exist, how do successful caregivers manage this paradox?"

The study results confirm my understanding of overcare. The study revealed that the nurses whose care turned into worry and anguish for their patients were the ones who burned out, feeling they just couldn't care anymore. *So the end result of overcare is a shortage of true care.* Let me further summarize Dr. Montgomery's findings. What emerged was that true care enabled nurses to manage and maintain a level of excellence and satisfaction with their work after many years in what would seem to most people an often demanding and demoralizing job. Care includes *connection,* as distinguished from over-involvement, rescuing, or co-dependency, which are destructive for both the caregiver and the patient or client. Caring serves as a source of self-renewal, profound fulfillment, and growth rather than burnout. Dr. Montgomery reported that her findings are consistent with other research showing that it's not caring that leads to burnout, but the eventual *lack* of caring. Caring itself allows access to a very important source of energy and renewal.

CUT-THRU to Balanced Care

CUT-THRU technology can illustrate the patterns fatiguing the human system and how they dilute the effects of your intended care. It will show you how overcare causes *distortions in perception* resulting in stress. CUT-THRU offers a scientifically researched method to access heart intelligence to release overcare and find balanced care. Balanced care is essential to getting one's emotional, mental, and physical systems in sync and coherent. What would be *balanced care* for yourself, your family, your job, your community, or the world? Practicing CUT-THRU engages your heart intelligence to guide you in distinguishing the difference between overcare and balanced care within yourself.

If you want to care more about your health, you probably would begin with a genuine motive of care, but if you overcare you might go to unbalanced extremes and drain your system mentally, emotionally, and physically. Then your system has to generate extra energy to compensate, so caring for your health becomes a burden. Balanced care for health requires mental and emotional balance in your approach.

Families and children need balanced care to flourish and hold together. When a parent's care for a child turns into overcare, it drains the entire family. Parental overcare is commonly reflected in ongoing worries and anxieties about health, grades, who their children's friends are, what their future will be, and so forth. Children tend to shut out parents who are always overcaring, which leads to parental frustration and more overcare. Heart intelligence would advise you how to stop overcaring and have balanced care instead.

In the workplace, people upset and fatigue themselves daily with overcare. Many don't understand why they wake up tired, why they feel burdened by work, and why they never have enough time. Innocently, they've caught the social disease of overcare — a virus that has become so natural that people don't even know they have it because it postures itself as care. Don't think the small worries and anxieties that sap the quality of life as you go about your tasks are not worth doing something about. You'll be surprised at how much energy you'll save and how much happier and more effective you'll be on the job.

Some people care enough to devote time and energy to community issues. However, when there is emotional *over-identity* with a social cause, the feeling of care degrades to overcare. Social overcare results in angry exchanges and can even lead to violence. People overcaring about the same cause frequently conflict with each other — tensions run high when overcare's in town — thereby destroying their intended efforts. Overcare has become a cunning and rampant emotional virus derived from care.

Many who care about society find themselves saddened or angry watching the news. Not knowing what to do, they rail at the President, cry over the starving and abused, and fear the crime and violence. Responding to the world from overcare, they become emotionally drained, fail to sleep at night, and remain insecure. This accelerates hopelessness and aging. Most would say they are just caring and ask, "What else can I do?" By realizing it's overcare that is draining you and preventing clear perception of how to respond effectively to issues or problems, you can cut through to balanced care.

Genuine care is a powerful motivator. It revitalizes and balances the entire system, providing a sense of fulfillment and more textures of experience. Controlled studies with CUT-THRU described in Chapter 5 have shown that men and women can significantly increase genuine care, appreciation, love, forgiveness, harmony, and vigor in their lives. These powerful emotional states activate the nervous system's parasympathetic signals which protect the heart and enhance immune system functions.[6] Cutting-thru overcare feelings of worry, anxiety, insecurity, dread, fear, guilt, etc., creates changes in the feelings themselves, which brings you entirely new perspectives of your life.

Most of us have learned in school to develop the *intellect* but not the *intelligence* which includes feelings. Without feeling, the mind with all its reasoning and thinking ability is inadequate to assess human situations accurately. Working with thousands of people from all strata of society over the past twenty years, I have learned that the feeling world is critical to effective decision-making. Dr. Antonio Damasio, a neurologist whose laboratory is highly regarded worldwide, offers scientific verification of this. He researched the neural underpinnings of reason and found that when parts of the brain which integrate feelings and emotions with reason are damaged, then personal and social behavior are severely compromised, even though all the logical and other aspects of the mind are unaffected.[7]

CUT-THRU empowers you to discern the effects of your intended care and look after yourself, your job, and other people in a balanced way. It's regenerative for both you and the receiver. Balanced care is nurturing and creative, providing security and support for all involved. It supplies meaning to challenges and provides *hope* for yourself and others. Hope is the catalyst to improve life, both the inner and outer atmosphere. When enough people know how to effectively care and feel cared for, it could change the world. Balanced care is the hope for the global future and new millennium.

Sincerity

Sincerity is a powerful core heart feeling that amplifies coherence. Added to genuine care, it has the power to dissolve problems before they become extreme. Balancing your care begins with sincerity in your approach. It is the missing ingredient that can provide a more productive work, home, or community environment. A deeper, sincere, family-type of care opens the conduit for real hope to appear. Look around at our world. It's starving for sincere care, that's obvious. Webster's first definition of care, "a troubled or burdened state of mind," has become the rule. People have it backwards, and that's overcare.

As a society, we are beaten down by stress and have simply quit caring. When individuals begin to understand how to scientifically and genuinely care again — but without the stress and burnout of overcare — they will activate their heart intelligence. Then the problems of violence, homelessness, racial inequality, the economy, health care, divorce, and child abuse can start to resolve. However, social change has to start with you, the individual, first.

Chapter 2

A 24-Hour Profile

For most people, life has become increasingly hectic. The number one stress complaint I hear is, *"There's too much to do and not enough time and energy to get it all done."* When "to-do" lists pile up, you're rushing to tie up loose ends, and you feel you're carrying more than your share of the load, overcare and stress mount. If you experience five stressful incidents in one day, that may not seem too bad. However, five stresses a day for five days in a row equals twenty-five compound stresses. After a while, that ratio takes its toll.

Research has shown that stressful feelings trigger changes in hormones throughout the body.[8] Hormones are chemical messengers that regulate most of the body's functions, including the way the brain processes information. Cortisol is called a "stress hormone" because it rises when we feel stress, especially emotional stress such as irritation, frustration, worry, anxiety, or anger. The effects of these stressful emotions accumulate and result in disorganized, or incoherent, flows of internal energy. Your system has to work harder to recover and regain balance. For many, the tension-filled days never stop. People care so much in their effort to keep up, it can feel like being on an endless treadmill.

A Hectic Day in Life

Let's take a look at a hectic day in the life of a working mother. Ann has three children, a husband, and a full-time job. Millions of people have much more difficult situations than Ann's and often experience challenges that are as hard or even harder. At work Ann supervises twelve people on a product design team and her decisions affect them all. This morning she received word that her boss Phil was unhappy with her last project. Apparently, Phil did not like the extra spending that was involved in the project design and implementation. Ann's team had felt the extra spending was necessary to insure safety and reliability, and Ann had approved it. She's just heard that the project might be reassigned to another team.

Ann's emotions flare up. Sitting at her desk trying to hold back her hurt and anger, Ann's stomach churns, her face is flushed, and she can't concentrate. After hours of worrying and feeling nauseous, she has to get away and leaves at 4:00 p.m., hoping a walk on the beach will calm her down and help her think straight. The afternoon sun sparkles on the water, but overcare thoughts keep flying through Ann's mind, "I was just caring about the product, the customer, and the company! Phil doesn't understand. This is the last time; I'm tired of caring. It's just not worth it." The walk isn't working. Ann gets more upset and tears roll down her cheeks. She barely notices the beach. Everything at work has backfired and Ann is so hurt she doesn't care anymore. She stomps her foot on some seaweed and begins to feel numb as if every ounce of feeling in her heart has shut down. In despair, she gives up and starts back to the car.

In the parking lot, Ann runs across an old friend she hasn't seen in months. Just seeing Donna brings a little life back to Ann's heart. As they talk, Donna's voice starts to tremble, "I just learned that my husband received a job offer after three months of being out of work. Now we'll be able to keep our home." Hearing Donna's story brings a caring feeling back to Ann's heart and the two share a few tears of release together. Ann heads for her car. The black cloud of worry and despair has lifted, and a feeling of appreciation for her own job begins to take hold. During the drive she starts to smile, remembering how enthusiastically everyone on her staff had responded to the new project. She thinks, "I'll just have to be more skillful in communicating with Phil, explain our design plans earlier, get his buy-in up front. My team is worth it and I'll find a way to look after them and work with Phil."

Feeling better, she arrives at the store to buy groceries but the checkout line is a mile long. She looks at her watch. "It's already 6:00 p.m. Now supper's going to be late," Ann sighs. Then she remembers that her husband Tom has to eat early because of a 7:00 p.m. meeting. Her feelings swiftly shift to overcare. She taps her foot nervously as she waits in line at the cash register, wishing everyone would just hurry up. The woman at the front of the line pulls out a check that needs the store manager's approval. Ann's irritation mounts. The next person's credit card won't go through the machine and he doesn't have the cash, further delaying the line's movement. Frustrated, Ann curses the store for not having more clerks to help. On the drive home, she resumes her anxious thoughts of how late supper will be. She's totally lost the warm feeling she had after talking to Donna. Her anxiety about her boss and what people will think of her resumes.

Ann passes some homeless people on the street. Momentarily, she feels compassion and then realizes,

"Well, at least I have a job, a home, and supper to cook, even if it is going to be late!" But as soon as she enters the house, there's Tom, frantic about his supper. Ann feels like she can't do anything right. After a bowl of cold cereal, Tom slams the door and leaves in a huff. Ann's insecure feelings keep recycling. Dinner is chaotic with the kids fighting over which video they're going to watch. Ann throws a load of dirty clothes in the machine, feeling guilty about Tom. Then the phone rings. It's her mother-in-law, Mary, who starts off complaining, as usual. Ann listens, but is now totally drained and cannot find an ounce of tolerance to buffer the irritation of the phone call. She wishes her mother-in-law would just disappear and leave them alone.

As Ann cleans up the dishes, one of the kids bumps her arm and a couple of plates clatter to the floor. Ann flies off the handle, slaps him in anger and sends him to his room. With this last straw she forgets the dishes, gets into her pajamas and crawls into bed. Feelings of insecurity and self-blame for how she's handling the kids wash over her and she cries herself to sleep.

The morning finds Ann exhausted and a stony silence prevalent in the house. She drives to work, but an empty sense of hopelessness surrounds her. A co-worker, Jean, notices her swollen eyes and asks kindly how she is. Ann breaks down. She needs help. She needs sincere care.

This not untypical 24-hour profile exemplifies how swiftly feelings can shift. Look at most people's fast-paced lives. One minute they care and feel good, the next minute they're in overcare and stress, bouncing up and down like a yo-yo. As overcare dominates, the yo-yo finally goes limp and you have to rewind it. So if you care, how do you keep overcare thoughts and feelings from dragging you down until you reach the end of your rope? Ann bounced back once or twice during that 24-hour period. But the next event would send her back down again. Multitudes of people don't know how to stop this yo-yo effect.

Stopping Overcare

Stopping the yo-yo effect requires transforming stressful reactions into an opportunity for empowerment and balanced care. Look at caring energy as if it were a bank account, one that starts out each day with energy to use in any way you choose. As with most accounts, you make withdrawals and deposits. This particular account is controlled by a computer that is directly linked to your mind and emotions. Thoughts and feelings affect how your energy is spent. Overcare thoughts and feelings cause a deficit, while caring or appreciative feelings regenerate the energy supply.

An important factor in stopping the yo-yo effect is understanding that when you make a conscious effort to find balance in a stressful situation, you add energy to your account. As the overcare feeling diminishes, perception becomes clearer. If you then increase caring and appreciative feelings, you add interest to your account. Eventually you can accumulate so much energy and get so rich that your bank account no longer needs to be a matter of daily concern.

Here's an example of how it works. The next morning when the alarm goes off, Ann reaches out and hits the "snooze" button, then rolls over dreading another day. If we could see the computer readout and what Ann's just done to her energy supply, the dread registers as a deficit. You could say the feeling of dread is so strong that it drained maybe ten points of energy. "Beeeeeeep!"

With the second alarm, Ann wonders, "Why hasn't Tom gotten up yet? It's his day to shower first." She reaches over and shakes him. "Five more minutes, please, I got in late," he mutters. Well, Ann's irritated now, as it seems this happens every morning of her life. With these thoughts stirring up old judgments, she's probably used up another five points of energy.

Ann gets out of bed and heads off to the kitchen to make breakfast. On the way, she grumbles about why mornings always feel so awful. Ann had recently heard about a new tool that's supposed to work right away to help you feel better. She ordered the book, which arrived a week ago, but hasn't had time to look at it. "I wonder what I did with that book," Ann thinks to herself. At that point Ann notices the cat asleep on the new couch and just can't believe it! "I've told those kids if they want to play with her in the evenings, then they have to remember to put her out!" She steps into a moist pile left by the cat. That does it! She screams upstairs for someone to get down and clean it up. Her computer readout clicks away at least fifteen points on this one. Finally she makes her way to the study where she finds the CUT-THRU book on a pile of other mail she hasn't had time to read.

For Ann, like many people, mornings are the most vulnerable times for negative thoughts and feelings to take hold. She's already created energy deficits and hasn't even gotten through breakfast! How you feel at the end of a day, a week, or a year, isn't just the result of chance. It can be "put a little in, take a lot away" all day long. With this kind of accumulated banking over 365 days a year, it doesn't take a genius to compute the results: extreme wear and tear mentally, emotionally, and physically. The human system is a complex and sensitive instrument. Over time it can break down. But you can also recharge it quickly once you know how. Batteries can lay drained for months, but plug them into the right recharger and they come back fast and work like new again.

Ann decides to let the kids make their own breakfast so she can try out CUT-THRU. She closes the door to the family room and goes right to the tool. She tries Steps 1 and 2. After a few minutes, Ann feels a peaceful feeling of balance and decides to enjoy her day. She gains an immediate twenty points of energy. To her surprise, getting the kids off to school flows smoothly. At work, everything goes well, that is, until Phil steps into her office to remind her to do something about her department's spending. The hurt feelings from the other day flood back. She stops and does Step 1 of CUT-THRU. She remembers how much she appreciates the people in her department and their great attitudes. She realizes that Phil is under a great deal of pressure from the president of the company. This perception surprises her; she hadn't realized until this moment just how much pressure Phil was under. Ann finds herself feeling compassion for him. Wanting to help him feels good again and she feels released from the overcare about her job that she's had for the past few days. Her energy is recharged and renewed.

Ann's impressed. The way she feels now is such a contrast to her last few days. She feels empowered and hopeful. As she continues playing with Step 1 and 2 throughout the day, cutting through her perceptions and reactions, she's shocked at how much her energy fluctuates with each overcare or judgment. By plugging all those energy drains, she's generated more points — and accumulated more energy — than she has spent by the end of the workday. Incidents that would have bumped her yesterday seemed like no big deal today. She even solved a departmental budgeting problem that had been wearing her down for weeks.

As you practice CUT-THRU, you'll discover new peace and creative insights on how to handle the ups and downs of daily life. Each challenge provides you with an opportunity to re-balance your care, gain a fresh perspective, and find a new solution. It becomes fun to CUT-THRU, just like learning to twirl a yo-yo can be fun once you get good at it. You'll create slick moves throughout the changing events in life and never have to reach the end of your rope.

All people naturally care. It's obvious in children. As they play they care. But when life beats and bangs with no release or reinforcement of true care, then overcares stack. As children grow older, their heads fill with the "cares" of the world — worries, anxieties, judgments, anger, depression, even hatred. The heart shuts down so they end up with no care. Going through the paces of surviving is all they can do. Many teenagers feel this way today. Everything becomes a grind. It's you against life. You feel like a walking statue made of stone. Multitudes of people end up at this point, but they don't have to. There is another choice.

Chapter 3

What's Behind Cᴜᴛ-Tʜʀᴜ?

So what's behind this tool that can help you re-generate care and nourish the system with balance and insight? *Caring for yourself!* In order to sustain care and understanding, you need to make a commitment to yourself. Quality care trusts and seeks resolutions for the prosperity of all involved. Before we describe the steps of Cᴜᴛ-Tʜʀᴜ in the next chapter, it's important to understand what's involved in achieving quality care.

A Bottom-Line – Caring For Yourself

Time and again, people lack the knowledge and tools to take care of self. Yet, they strain to care for the people and events in their lives. How can anyone genuinely care for others if they are anxious, worried, or depressed? I've participated in anxiety-driven care — concerning work, family, my own research into the nature of stress, long hours serving others, then tossing in bed restless and worried at night. I thought I was fine, doing what I was supposed to do, and that life was *just this way.* I read dietary labels and exercised regularly, yet I knew I was not that happy and didn't know why. I finally realized that in caring for everyone and everything else, I'd ignored areas within myself that needed attention and care.

There are various reasons why people don't care for themselves. Many become so identified with career, children, projects, making money, etc., they feel they have no time for themselves. They ignore or bury inner promptings regarding their own needs. Caring for self is the last thing they'll do until exhaustion or illness forces the issue. In the March 6, 1995 issue of *Newsweek*, the feature story was "Exhaustion — The Breaking Point." *Newsweek* explained that the fatigue of the '90s is the kind that a weekend's rest or reading on the beach can't cure. The article goes on to say that the technology boom offers no down time, no escape from work or people — we have cell phones in our cars and beepers in our pockets, and we carry them on vacation and to the bathroom. The tyranny of time demands continual rushing, accompanied by a feeling that we'll never get it all done. Companies now routinely ask one employee to do the work of 1.3 people, for the same pay, and with less time off. "Time has become an even more valued commodity than money," says *Newsweek*.

The article goes on to say that the stress toll on women tends to eclipse that of men. "Women are so good at guilt and guilt is exhausting." When women aren't perfect at both work and home, they tend to drive themselves off the edge. The Annals of Internal Medicine reported that 24% of women complain of fatigue that lasts longer than two weeks, and fatigue is now among the top reasons people call the doctor.[9]

Some people literally worry themselves to death. Japanese call worrying or stressing oneself until death "karoshi," which literally means dropping dead at your desk.[10] "Karoshi" has reached epidemic proportions in modern Japanese society. Americans may not be dying at their desks in significant numbers, but the stresses that leave us exhausted have been linked to health problems ranging from high blood pressure to poor immune system health. The bottom-line is this: As people deplete their energy without caring for themselves, they have no care left to give. I am not trying to paint a picture of gloom, I'm trying to clarify the facts and offer significant new hope.

What's at the Core of Overcare?

Overcare is as old as history and the cause of endless suffering. What's at the core of the problem is human perception and emotion, and the human reactions to perceptions and emotions, and so history repeats itself.

We all seem to know what emotions are until we try to define them. It's our emotional experience — the joys, the sorrows, the fun, the love — that makes us human and more than machines. The quest to understand emotions has stumped scientists and philosophers for centuries. Aristotle believed that emotions were experienced in the heart and this view prevailed for hundreds of years. In fact, it's in the area of the heart where people experience the physical feeling of many emotions, so it was natural to assume that the heart was the source.

Science Tries to Understand Emotion

With the popularity of scientific reductionism during the past few centuries, the human body has been divided into pieces to understand how each part of the body mechanically functions. It was discovered that a section deep in the brain's limbic system, the amygdala, specializes in memories of fear while the intellectual memory of emotions is routed through the hippocampus. The prefrontal cortex of the brain, essential to decision-making, also processes emotional experience. When parts of the brain are removed or damaged in older children or adults, certain emotions are no longer experienced.[7] Therefore, many scientists concluded that emotions originate only in the brain. They also believe that emotions are *only* created through biochemistry. This would imply that we have no choice over our emotions. However, the brain's electrical and biochemical changes very often occur in *response* to feelings and perceptions over which we do have *choice*, and the heart is very much involved in the process.

Feelings can happen much faster than thought. Daniel Goleman, author of the ground-breaking book *Emotional Intelligence,* points out, "For decades it was thought all information from the senses went first to the neo-cortex, where it was understood, and only then to the amygdala, where an emotional response was added.[11,12] Only recently have neuroscientists discovered a brain circuit that lets a signal of what we see and hear go straight to the amygdala without passing through the rational decision-making of the neo-cortex. That lets the amygdala set its response in motion (based on past memories of distress) even though it lacks the neo-cortex's perceptual accuracy. That's why we so often feel and act before we think," Goleman explains. However, he goes on to say, "Brain circuits continue to be shaped by experiences throughout life. It's never too late for us to learn — or to change." I have found *the heart* to be the most powerful change agent — the key to developing emotional intelligence and perceptual accuracy.

Why do we try to teach children to manage their feelings and emotional reactions? Parenting is raising a child to take care of himself. Yet few of us have learned how to effectively parent our own emotions and perceptions. Nevertheless, society calls us "grown up" when our physical bodies reach maturity around age eighteen.

In my view, "grown up" is indicated by mental and emotional maturity in caring for self. Generating care oils the entire system. Just as a car engine needs oil for all the parts to run smoothly, so does the human system need the lubricating power of care. Spirit manifests as true care, a textured feeling in the core of the heart, and the doorway to a higher dimension of both perception and feeling.

It's one thing to understand that perceptions and emotions are at the core of the problem of overcare; it's quite another thing to know what to do about it. One's perceptions and feelings are one's truth, or reality, in the moment and can change in the next moment. When you judge or over-react to a perception, you assign emotional energy to that perception, energizing that particular view of reality. Learning to perceive a broader reality involves learning to parent your perceptions and emotions without overcare, judgments, and blame. Intelligent understanding of any situation demands the harmonious integration of both heart and mind to give you the widest possible picture of reality. With hindsight, we often see life more accurately. How many times have people wished that they'd done something differently because they see more clearly now! The trick is learning to bring that hindsight into your present moment.

Overcare, negativity, and self-judgment result from people's inability to emotionally manage themselves in the moment and perceive intuitively from the heart. With the impact of increased information in today's world, the mind and emotions quickly become over-stimulated and stressed as they try to process all the incoming data. This stops intuition. *Heart perception* brings balance to information processing even while it ushers in broader perspectives and intuitive understanding. One intuition can cut through analyzing hundreds of pages of information. The joint venture between heart and mind gives human beings the power to adapt, manage emotions and perceptions, and make decisions that are the best for themselves and the whole. As you develop the heart's intelligence, when challenges arise, you realize that you do have a conscious *choice* in how to perceive them.

Hormonal Effects of Overcare

It's challenging enough to try to decipher what to do with emotions or perceptions while we are experiencing them. But as unresolved feelings and memories pile up, hormonal imbalances result, making us highly vulnerable to perceiving future situations with a slant of worry, anxiety, frustration, anger, etc. Our biochemistry is then working against us, amplifying emotional reactiveness and warping our perceptions.

Stress feelings can often dominate our reality, although that is not their intended purpose. They are designed to be warning signals telling us something is out of balance and needs adjusting, often in our attitude or approach to a situation. As we recognize stress feelings as flag warnings, rather than as suffering in themselves, we can do something productive with them. If we don't know how to address a stress signal, the nervous and hormonal systems will automatically go into a primitive "fight or flight" reaction as if you were in real danger.[13] Many people have become so habituated to stress reactions, they don't recognize them as stress anymore. They live with a low-grade anxiety or depression and don't even know it's there. Yet, the body pays the price. A fish living in polluted water has no idea there are other fish living in fresh, clean water or even that fresh water exists. Such is the power of our habituated stress reactions. Yet, if a current of fresh water were to flow in, the fish would race to it. Such is the power of your heart intelligence to release stress and bring you back into "flow."

Most drivers have had near-miss accidents where they slammed on the brakes and narrowly avoided hitting another car. The stress reaction depletes their energy in a few seconds, but it can take hours for the body to fully recover. If there is habitual overcare, the constant release of stress hormones accumulates in the body. For many, overcare accumulates into pain, often a headache or backache, before they recognize there's a problem. For others, overcare stacks to the point of explosion, as it did with Ann slapping her child. If you allow overcare to continue to stack, you eventually have exhaustion, unsoundness, collapse, and breakdown. Unresolved overcare can contribute to many illnesses, including anxiety disorders, depression, cancer, heart disease.

Female and Male Hormonal Imbalances

A single event that triggers nervous system or hormonal system imbalance can spawn emotional vulnerability. When emotionally vulnerable, situations you thought you had already made peace with can resurge and once again drain your system. A woman's monthly period — when the hormonal balance naturally changes — is a time when women need to be extra watchful of overcare. Even knowing "the time is at hand" is not enough to stave off the strong premenstrual syndrome (PMS) emotional reactions common to many women. Similar hormonal imbalances and emotional vulnerability can occur after childbirth, at puberty, and during menopause. Overcare at menses, childbirth, or menopause strongly amplifies the hormonal imbalance. In cases of anorexia (a common overcare-related eating disorder in adolescent girls), pituitary hormones that affect sexuality become deficient. Menstruation may cease. As overcare generates chronic imbalances between the hormones estrogen and progesterone, then extreme anxiety, irritation, over-sensitivity, panic attacks, or depression can result. Each year 40 million Americans experience some degree of depression and two-thirds of them are women.[14] One in five women have a history of depression. Under emotional stress, progesterone converts to adrenaline. Over-production of adrenaline leads to bursts of activity, followed by fatigue, emotional instability, lack of mental clarity, a decrease in personal effectiveness, physical ailments, lack of hope, and accelerated aging.

Since males do not have monthly periods, male hormones, such as testosterone, have a more continuous pattern. Unbalanced testosterone levels can make males highly aggressive and reactive. Testosterone deficiency may result in instability and insecurity in men or passive/aggressive behavior. As stress mounts in today's society, we see renewed indications of testosterone imbalances in men — increased physical aggression, violence, rape, sado-masochism, and a culture of abuse. According to a recent report, "If you look at a sample of college students, where they've been steadily dating for at least three months, you now see physical aggression rates of 30-35%."[15]

Overcare and the Heart

The physical heart is also extremely taxed by overcare-induced stress. In fact, scientific research now shows anxiety to be one of the strongest risk factors for sudden cardiac arrest, up to six times more than cigarette smoking or other known risk factors.[16] Heart disease has become the number one killer in both men and women in industrialized nations. The American Heart Association estimates that more than one in four

Americans over age eighteen have hypertension (high blood pressure), a precursor to heart disease, and that 40 million Americans suffer from diseases of the heart and blood vessels.[17] When men or women experience stress, the sympathetic branch of the autonomic nervous system is activated. Under chronic stress, the sympathetic stays over-stimulated, a common symptom of "Type A" behavior, characterized by impatience, anger, hostility, and increased risk of heart arrhythmia.[18] Stressful feelings also stimulate steroid secretions from the adrenal cortex which in turn stimulate corticosteroids which increase glucose production. Extra glucose is converted to fat to protect the body. This is how stress can cause excessive fat build-up in the coronary arteries.

Compassion

The role of hormones in health, disease, and aging is a growing area of medical research. Millions of baby boomers are now in their forties and half of them will soon enter the hormonal "change of life" called menopause. Compassion is tremendously important in balancing one's perceptions, emotions, and hormones. Scientific research has shown that feelings of compassion and care not only create coherent heart frequencies that help balance the hormonal system, they also enhance the immune system.[19] People of all ages need compassion and tools to manage their emotions in today's rapidly changing world. As the pace of life speeds up, it doesn't take much for feelings to intensify quickly. Once people see what's behind overcare and gain a deeper understanding of its perceptual, emotional, and physiological causes, they need to know how to self-correct.

How CUT-THRU Works

CUT-THRU shows you how to self-correct distortions

in perceptions, emotions, and their hormonal consequences. As you release overcares, you find new freedom.
Although a surprise or a shock could disrupt anyone's
system for a while, with practice of the tool, even in extreme stress you can find a peaceful equilibrium and
quickly recoup the energy loss. It's worth the investment
of time and slows the aging process in many areas of
your system.

Self-correction starts with being aware that feelings
of insecurity, anxiety, guilt, anger, or regret, can come and
go like the tides. People tend to habitually analyze, vent,
or repress these feelings in an effort to get rid of them.
This rarely works. Others say they use fretting, anxiety,
anger, or regret, to motivate themselves to work harder
or perform better. The problem is these feelings all produce *incoherence* in the human system which actually
hinders performance and drains your vitality. As you
practice CUT-THRU, you learn to use anxiety or any stress
signal to go deeper in the heart to find balance and understanding. This stops ineffective mental rendering and
releases the disturbed feeling, so you can find the intuitive flow state that leads to peak performance. It does
this by helping you see the difference between *lower heart
feelings* that cause overcare and *higher heart feelings* of
genuine care within yourself. Understanding this distinc-
tion is at the core of CUT-THRU technology.

Lower and Higher Heart Feelings

Sentiment, attachment, expectation, and sympathy
are what I call lower heart feelings. When you experience lower heart feelings, the mind and heart are out of
sync and often in conflict. The mind pulls your energy
out of the heart and into the solar plexus where you feel
the overcare. Lower heart feelings can be tough to release because there is still some heart energy or care in

them. However, higher heart feelings are what quickly re-align the heart and mind to give you emotional release and hope. Your care becomes regenerated. Genuine love, care, appreciation, and compassion are higher heart feelings that activate heart intelligence. Through practicing CUT-THRU, you transform lower heart feelings and become the architect of higher heart feelings of hope and power within yourself.

Let's look at how it works. "Sentiment" is when you have a thought, attitude, or feeling toward someone or something that's influenced by tender emotions. So why is being sentimental a lower heart feeling? When a tender feeling turns sentimental, like remembering a time you spent with someone and missing that feeling, the sense of loss can pull your heart into sadness and sorrow. You can also feel sentimental toward yourself. If you are overweight but dwell on memories of when you could fit into a size six dress, the sentiment can turn into despair. It's not the memory itself that drains you, but the overcare thoughts and feelings associated with the memory that bring sadness and heartache. As soon as you recognize an overcare feeling or thought, try to activate a higher heart feeling instead. This allows you quick access to new perception and intelligence.

For example, if you feel sentimental about missing a loved one and start to get upset, try to find a feeling of appreciation for the time you had together. As you add energy to that higher heart feeling, your intuition becomes activated. It will guide you to a new attitude or insight that feels good to your spirit. You stop the drain of overcare and find creative care. Higher heart feelings generate the coherent heart frequencies that are access codes to your spirit. Even if you don't see an immediate solution, you renew your energy, strength, and sense of security.

"Attachment" is another lower heart feeling. Being attached is a feeling that binds you to a person, place, thing, or idea to the extent that you lose balanced perspectives. A mother has a natural feeling of attachment to her child. However, if she attaches herself to the point where she can't bear to be apart from the child, attachment builds dependency, reinforcing her own and her child's insecurity and unhappiness.

People also build attachments to thoughts and habits. Some feel they must have their morning cup of coffee, or fold the clothes a certain way, or insist their beliefs are right. They become so set in their ways they lose flexibility. What doesn't flex eventually breaks. It isn't people, places, thoughts, or issues that break your heart. It's attachment. Attachment narrows perspective and victimizes *you*. If your attachment to something or someone is causing your overcare, try to find balanced care perspectives. With practice, you can CUT-THRU any insecurity or fear associated with attachment and discover real freedom.

"Expectation" is another lower heart feeling. People care, therefore they expect others to behave a certain way and are disillusioned if they don't act accordingly. Expectation is the emotional investment in an idea. That investment sets you up for disappointment. All of us have some expectations, so compassion for oneself is important. Learn to distinguish between fun *expectancies* and emotional *expectations*. You can have a fun expectancy that your family will enjoy a new recipe you spent hours preparing, but you won't be devastated if they dislike it. Emotional expectations of wives, husbands, children, or events, are what commonly set us up for hurt, anger, or betrayal. As we become drained by repeated disappointment, true care and love are lost. By learning how to understand and manage your expectations, you can love and not keep getting disappointed.

Often our greatest expectations are of ourselves. Perfectionism and performance anxiety are key stressors that undermine our happiness. We expect ourselves to live up to our images and ideals and feel guilty when we don't. A friend of mine valiantly set out to take care of his health. He planned a low-fat diet and bought an expensive rowing machine. Five days later he still hadn't used the machine and blew his diet with a chocolate mousse he just couldn't refuse. His self-care turned to overcare and guilt about not achieving his own expectations. Fun expectancies encourage us to keep trying, but idealistic expectations undermine attempts to care for ourselves. CUT-THRU can help you release perfectionism and find balanced care instead. It's a happier and more productive approach to a quality life.

"Sympathy" is also a lower heart feeling. Sympathy is sharing in another's sadness. It's tricky because it seems like caring; however, sympathetic feelings of sadness diminish your ability to care. When you sympathize, you are commiserating with another person's stress. Before you know it, you are consumed with overcare and now you have two pitiful people instead of one. Compassion is the higher heart feeling that lifts us out of the stress brought on by sympathy. Compassion helps you feel what it's like to walk in someone's shoes, but know when to stop so you don't walk off a cliff with them. A buddy once described sympathy to me like this: "If a bucket has a hole in it and all its water is leaking out, it doesn't help to punch a hole in your own bucket." Sympathy bleeds your energy; compassion accumulates energy and provides productive insight.

The "Poor-Me's"

We end up in a state of **poor-me** when we sympathize with our own problems. Self-sympathy is agreeing with our overcare, justifying that we should or even MUST feel worried, sad, or stressed. As self-pity occupies your mind, it blocks out solutions. A friend of mine wondered how she was going to pay for needed dental work and found herself worrying about money. As she sympathized with her worried thoughts, her self-care quickly turned to self-pity and she became emotionally distraught. She no longer had any energy to find a solution. If she had known how to CUT-THRU to a higher heart feeling of compassion for herself, it would have empowered her creative care to find a solution.

Left unchecked, the "poor-me's" can cascade into depression. A business associate was in a relationship that ended unpleasantly. He spent weeks in self-pity until he realized the woman wasn't right for him. He decided to put all his energy into a challenging goal at work but didn't feel appreciated by management for his efforts and felt sorry for himself. One evening, while searching for something in a drawer, he found an old photograph of the two of them and all the old hurt and poor-me feelings about the relationship flooded back. He stayed depressed for months. This example illustrates how only one incident that again initiates feeling sorry for yourself can twist a true perception you already had about a previous situation in your life.

As you practice CUT-THRU, you increase the power of self-care so you can completely recover from challenging times in life. This tool enables you to adapt and stop the energy drain, then gain the insight and understanding you need to get your life back together quickly. It does this by showing you how to find a sense of peace and a higher heart feeling which activates a pathway from the heart to higher perceptual centers of the brain. This harmonizing of heart and mind is what brings intuitive heart perception which releases the overcare.

The Power of Love

Higher heart feelings are love. They are different from mushy, sentimental overcare feelings that are associated with the lower heart. Higher heart feelings create access to new intelligence. Mental or emotional intelligence alone provides partial perspectives. Only the central heart intelligence organizes information from the entire system in the intuitive domain, then provides perspectives that are based on true care for all. Within the heart are the higher aspects of the human spirit — genuine love, care, appreciation, compassion, patience, humor, courage, forgiveness, security, and kindness. These qualities of spirit are the power of the heart. They are what make life worth living. Without them, we go through the motions of survival living, victims of mental disarray and emotional starvation. Scientific research is showing that these higher heart qualities are what create order and balance in the electrical frequencies and rhythms of the heart, brain, nervous system, and cells and can be accessed to rejuvenate you throughout day-to-day activities. *That's what they are for.* Higher heart feelings are the true fountain of youth. Practicing CUT-THRU will give you the power to keep higher heart feelings regenerating your system, enhancing your passion to care, and unfolding a new love for life. Eventually you will no longer need to practice the tool and will stay naturally in the flow of higher heart feelings and perceptions throughout the day and night. Life can still be life, but you'll have the flexibility and know-how to go back to the higher heart if a stressor gets to you and the power to CUT-THRU.

Chapter 4

The Steps of CUT-THRU

The CUT-THRU technique is progressive — you use only the steps you need. After you become familiar with the process, Step 1 is often all you'll need to find relief. *Step 1 becomes more powerful as you gain understanding of the shift it offers.* In more difficult situations, you will need to go through all five steps to experience total release. Terms like rain, float, and fair heart are fully explained in the next few pages. Remembering these key terms is a short cut, like using a command key on a computer. One command brings up the whole program to quickly shift you back into a *flow,* regenerating your energy and intuitive intelligence.

Here are the five steps of CUT-THRU.

Step 1. **Recognize feelings and thoughts of overcare — Take an inner weather report. See if your inner weather is rain or sunshine. Then change your weather to prevent a flood. Choose the more hopeful perspective.**

Step 2. **Hold overcare thoughts or feelings in the heart. Remember, adapting stops the energy drain. Pretend you are floating on a raft or soaking in a** heartwarming bath for a few moments. If the disturbed feelings won't release, or if your emotions are really revved up, homogenizing or blending the feelings in the heart helps the energy disperse so you can see a new perspective.

Step 3. Find your peace. As the current of discomfort dissipates, a new sense of peace and intuitive knowing can emerge. Hold to any feeling of peace. Then go to the "fair heart" to see and reflect clearly.

Step 4. Find the reference point of care. Ask yourself, "Why did I originally care?" Recall those beginning feelings of care for a few moments. Then ask yourself, "How did my original care slowly leak away due to overcare and drain me?" Recognize how your care was taken to inefficient extremes. Recall the original care and find the higher heart perspective.

Step 5. Follow your heart intelligence. In this last step, with clear perception and feelings of security coming back, listen to your heart to know what *true care* would now be in this situation. Follow your true care. That's caring for self and others.

Now let's explain the purpose of each step and how to do it in more detail.

Step 1. Recognize feelings and thoughts of overcare — Take an inner weather report. See if your inner weather is rain or sunshine. Then change your weather to prevent a flood. Choose the more hopeful perspective.

Your inner weather is how good you feel in your heart — or not. Any uncomfortable feeling of unease, worry, anxiety, insecurity, etc., is overcare. It's time to CUT-THRU, stop the emotional wear and tear, and change your inner weather. If your inner weather is turbulent, you can't see past the storm inside. Start to notice how sentiments, expectations, attachments, and disappointments cloud your feelings and drain your power away until you feel like a victim. If you have a constant low-grade anxiety or uneasiness, your inner weather report is "partly cloudy." Most people are so used to partly cloudy being normal, it seems natural that the sun's never totally out. Overcare creates fog or clouds which obscure clear perception. Expectations of what should be different are mind attempts to change inner weather, but it won't change until people release the overcare.

Look at your thoughts and feelings as a barometer. If there's even one thing "wrong" and the mind overcares about it, then negative thoughts will rain. When it's raining, you often can't remember there's still a sun shining behind the clouds. Ask yourself, "Rain or Sunshine?" It's a quick way to decide which perspective to focus on. You need to choose sunshine, not just think about it, to CUT-THRU to a clear and wider view. New thoughts, feelings, and intelligence will follow your perception shift.

Practice Step 1 on small overcares first, such as feeling anxious while waiting for someone to finish talking, the worry you feel when a family member is late coming home, or the dread you feel at tax time. Then you'll be able to find relief from stronger overcares, such as the insecurity you feel when you hear someone close is not well. Here's an example: You hear that a friend is in the hospital. A feeling of unease arises and overcare thoughts commence: what if he dies, what will happen to his poor family, what about your friendship, and so on. Here's how to practice Step 1. Check your inner weather and recognize the uneasy feelings and worrisome thoughts clouding your mind. Ask yourself, "Rain or Sunshine?" If you go with "rain," your next thoughts will probably generate more fear or sadness and, if left unchecked, you'll soon be in despair. If you choose "sunshine," your next thoughts could generate appreciation for your friendship, a clear feeling of balanced care as you find out the facts of his situation, and clarity on what to do. Holding to appreciation provides regenerative energy and creative caring that can help.

Cutting-thru small day-to-day overcares recoups spent energy. It also gives you confidence to CUT-THRU the bigger overcares when they arise. Have patience with yourself. With a little practice you'll understand how it works. Often you may feel an uneasy feeling without even knowing why. Practice Step 1 and choose "sunshine." That can release the feeling to give you a smoother flow and a quick uplift. Choosing "sunshine" is not ignoring the problem. If there really is something wrong, it will become evident and you will have more clarity on what to do. If the feeling does not release, go to Step 2.

Step 2. **Hold overcare thoughts or feelings in the heart. Remember, adapting stops the energy drain. Pretend you are floating on a raft or soaking in a heartwarming bath for a few moments. If the disturbed feelings won't release, or if your emotions are really revved up, homogenizing or blending the feelings in the heart helps the energy disperse so you can see a new perspective.**

Floating in the heart releases over-identification with overcare feelings and helps you adapt. Try to relax any current of discomfort, find peace, and float in a "soft heart." The purpose of this step is not to repress uncomfortable feelings but to dissipate them. Most people have not been educated on how to release disturbed feelings and thoughts. Instead, they vent, analyze, or suppress them in the effort to get rid of them. None of these methods works in the long run. The stress still accumulates. Venting is less harmful to your body than repression. It can feel good for a moment; however, it still bleeds energy and never brings complete understanding of the situation you are venting about. Emotional venting is different from talking over a problem with someone, which your intuition may suggest you do.

Neutral

Holding overcare feelings and thoughts in the heart helps balance your nervous system and your hormonal system. Floating in neutral is a posture you can learn to access even amidst turbulence. The mind wants things to change and grows impatient when they don't. The heart adapts, recoups spent emotional energy, and builds power for things to change. Hold feelings of commotion in the heart for a few moments and relax. Allow intuition to casually float up from the heart into your awareness.

In the beginning of learning to CUT-THRU, you might tell yourself to stay neutral, but insecurity paralyzes you or the mind gets restless or bored and doesn't want to "do nothing." Going to neutral is like gear-shifting when you drive a car. Most people stay mentally and emotionally revved up, causing metal-on-metal grind, going from forward to reverse and back, forgetting to shift to neutral first. If you go to *neutral in the heart* first, you are more likely to know whether to shift into forward or reverse and at what speed to move, preventing wear and tear on your engine or a crash. You save energy, build flexibility, and slow the aging process.

Stirring the Feelings

Floating in the heart creates an emotionally-neutral state. But if the disturbed feelings won't release, or if your emotions are really revved up, homogenizing or blending the feelings in the heart helps the energy disperse so you can see new. It's like using a blender to stir, whip, puree, or liquefy the insecurity, worry, guilt, etc. The amplitude of blending has to be as strong as the overcare identity in order to release the residue feelings. If you hold to even a small feeling of peace, your spirit has a window to enter with a new ray of hope and intuitional understanding. Long-held hurt, emotional trauma, resentment, or guilt can be extremely difficult to release. As you practice Step 2, you can increase heart care for yourself by slowly increasing the speed of homogenizing those deep feelings in the heart.

Step 2 may produce a few tears or condense into a steam of negative feelings or thoughts as they leave your system. That's part of the process. Try not to identify with any negativity. A few tears from the heart as feelings release are much different from emotional "head" crying, which has a lot of anger, self-pity, and indignation mixed in. Notice the difference. It's obvious in young children. A disappointment can produce a little crying or become a total engagement in a long fuss or tantrum when a child cannot let go of what he or she wanted or expected. It's the same with adults, but CUT-THRU creates new appreciative understanding that wipes away tears of stress and disappointment.

Step 3. **Find your peace. As the current of discomfort dissipates, a new sense of peace and intuitive knowing can emerge. Hold to any feeling of peace. Then go to the "fair heart" to see and reflect clearly.**

As stress feelings leave your system, peace returns. At times the peace may be accompanied by an empty feeling. Hold to any peace you can find even if it is not a complete peace. It is your springboard to renewed energy and vitality. The more you practice, the stronger the texture of peace will become. With peace, your higher heart care comes back. Then hope and glimpses of solutions or understandings have a chance to appear. Step 3 is like looking into a pond. Until the emotions of the water are peaceful, it's hard to reflect from the fair heart and see clearly.

Fair Heart

Fair heart is self-reflection from the heart — not the mind. Mind reflection tends to go in circles and create emotional playouts which only feed hurt, anger, stress, and feeling victimized. Fair heart means being self-honest and fair as you *challenge the assumptions* behind your mind perceptions so you don't automatically buy into them. As you focus your energy in the area of the heart, recouping spent mental and emotional energy, the heart and brain can entrain to assess a situation fairly and with intuitive clarity. Fair heart reveals the bigger picture and opens the possibilities for selecting creative solutions — it's transformational. Without fairness of heart, the mind shows you only the little picture.

To find "fair heart," stay focused deep in the heart, holding your energy there to allow heart and mind to align, then ask yourself questions to find the bigger picture. Listen from the heart. Heart intuition can give you answers like a computer read-out on where, why, and what to do next. You see just the right action which is CUT-THRU and not cut-off from someone or some issue. You find common-sense care. Looking for fairness in heart perspectives is a power tool to educate yourself into heart perception instead of mind perception. It is *allowing* on many levels. Allowing yourself, allowing others, allowing life. This *allows* the bigger picture to emerge inside your reality.

Going Deeper in the Heart

It's sincerely trying to go deeper in the heart that gives you the power to neutralize ill-managed emotions which reinforce thoughts like, "No one understands me," "No one really cares." The deeper in the heart you go, the more you delay emotional or mental reactiveness and the more *flex* and *recoup* power you gain. Recuperation is a process — often long and slow— of cooperation between mind and heart until there is realignment. CUT-THRU is high speed recoup and cuts time. The more you practice, the easier it gets and the more capacity you have to feel good fast. If you already feel strong about yourself and are happy, through increasing your emotional management of subtle overcares, judgmentalness, and reactiveness, you will power up to a new level of coherence and creativity. Many people have emotional strength, integrity, and high degrees of self-management. This process can take you into new levels of management which would increase your creativity and potential talents. When emotions are in balance and aligned with your real heart, this frees energy to expand your talents and creativity.

The meaning of life is found in the deeper heart, which produces more love and intelligence, which results in nourishment from heart perception. That nourishment provides strength to all your cells. The mind will take you back into over-identity if you let it. Remember that over-identities all have attached emotional energy drains. So rejoice when you catch yourself so you don't age yourself by assigning drain to your cares. As you practice Step 3, notice the direction your next thoughts take. If they are higher heart thoughts, you'll find peace and intuitive insight. If the thoughts and feelings keep getting pulled back to lower heart feelings, overcare identities, and density, then move on to Step 4. Over-identities are constructed through habit and Step 4 will give you the additional understanding you need for release.

Step 4. **Find the reference point of care. Ask yourself, "Why did I originally care?" Recall those beginning feelings of care for a few moments. Then ask yourself, "How did my original care slowly leak away due to overcare and drain me?" Recognize how your care was taken to inefficient extremes. Recall the original care and find the higher heart perspective.**

This step is like using the remote on your VCR to rewind the movie of your life back to the original care. You recognize and appreciate that overcare originated from care — whether for someone, some situation, an experience in the past, or a care about the future. Original care connects you to your spirit, your higher heart, providing mental, emotional, and hormonal regeneration. From that reference point of original care you can gain an energy-efficient perspective and re-create the movie of your life anew. Here are the key elements of this step.

A) Begin by softly focusing in the heart. Ask yourself, why did you originally care? You are not asking for a why from the head but for an understanding from the heart. What were those beginning feelings of care? How did the flow of higher heart care get caught in the rip tides of lower care due to sentiment, expectations, attachments, disappointments, etc., so your original care slowly leaked away? Surrender to the beginning feeling of true care. This will shift your energy back to the higher heart and increase the depth field of intuitive perception. As overcare feelings release, new thoughts will naturally follow. In a sense, this step is like erasing the chalkboard of the past for a clear new perception or a quick understanding, so you get back to balanced care with passion.

B) To recognize how your caring was taken to inefficient extremes, stop and ask yourself these questions:

1. Where did the drain begin?

2. Did my care slip into worry, fear, and fretting, causing me to operate on raw nerve energy?

3. Was my care helpful for both myself and the other person or issue?

4. Was my caring stress-producing?

5. How could my care be truly efficient now?

Asking these questions will help you track overcare and over-identity back to where it started and become conscious of the sequence of events. It's like seeing different frames in the holographic movie of your life and recognizing how overcare floods into stress. As you become conscious of the process, you can change it. You step off the mental and emotional merry-go-round. When you perceive how overcare slipped into worry and drained you until you were running on raw nerve energy, you perceive how you became a powerless victim of your own care. If our character Ann had known this CUT-THRU step earlier and tracked her overcare about her job back to the point it began, she would have recalled it was with her boss. She cared about her work and felt the boss didn't care and might reassign her project. She would have seen how overcare wasn't helpful to herself or to the team she cared about. In this step, she would have asked herself how her care could be more energy-efficient so that next time she wouldn't put herself through all that agony.

As you practice Step 4, it's important to remind yourself to stay with the original feeling of care. This stops the overcare from returning. If you give renewed energy to overcare thoughts, you re-create the same old movie. It takes practice to hold to balanced care to gain an energy-efficient perspective, but it feels great and regenerates the entire system. You learn that following what feels good to your heart brings empowering results. If your overcare has stacked for a time, it's been sincerely hard on your feelings. Have compassion for yourself and patience as you practice. Know your root motive to care was right; your head just took you off in the wrong direction. Knowing that is loving yourself!

Step 5. **Follow your heart intelligence. In this last step, with clear perception and feelings of security coming back, listen to your heart to know what *true care* would now be in this situation. Follow your true care. That's caring for self and others.**

Your heart intelligence comes to you as new perceptions and hope. It's important to deeply listen to and follow even fleeting heart perceptions. If a perception is peaceful and feels good to you, that's your signal to follow it. The heart signal is often weaker than the mind at first, so you have to listen deeply. Follow the heart, and watch your life unfold into a smoother, happier flow.

After you do all five steps, if there is still some cellular residue of overcare, rise above it, and appreciate the new that you have seen. Please don't judge yourself. As you appreciate and continue to follow your heart, life will unfold the complete release. You'll re-create the movie of your life, from the reference point of true care, creating a better outcome.

Eventually, all you will need to remember are the key terms in each step:

Step 1. **Check your inner weather — "Rain or Sunshine?"**

Step 2. **Adapt to stop the energy drain. "Float, soak, or blend" feelings in the heart.**

Step 3. **Find "Fair Heart."**

Step 4. **Recall "Original Care" or go to deeper neutral to save energy until you can find a "Higher Heart Feeling."**

Step 5. **"Follow your Heart Intelligence" — Using Heart Intelligence connects you with intuitive insight and rebuilds mental and emotional energy reservoirs.**

Set Up a Program to Practice CUT-THRU

In learning any skill, the more you do it, the easier it becomes. When people first learn how to use a computer, they learn how to turn it on, how to type, and how to access the programs. For awhile, their typing is slow, they miss keys, and aren't sure which commands to use. After some practice, they can type and switch programs without having to think about it. It's the same with CUT-THRU. Just keep using the steps sincerely. Your higher heart care will provide you with unfolding intelligence on how to adhere to balance.

Start to practice on small overcares to observe the perceptual shift that occurs. Watch how your perception can swiftly change when higher heart feelings of balanced care, appreciation, compassion, and love are re-kindled. You'll build your power to access higher heart feelings quickly and find relief even if a major stressor occurs. Cutting-thru old patterns and unproductive feelings saves wear and tear on your system and slows the aging process. Your spirit is regenerated. This is practical prevention for anxiety, depression, exhaustion, and burnout. As you become accustomed to the internal state of heart-mind entrainment, you learn to find a liquid flow through life and, even in challenging times, acquire intuitive insight.

Identify your overcares by asking yourself questions about people, places, things, or issues you care about. Ask yourself, *"Is my care stress-producing or stress-reducing?"* Check your inner weather for the answer — how good you feel in the heart or not. Take a moment now. Stop and sincerely ask yourself, "Is anything I care about causing me uneasiness, worry, anxiety, stress, guilt?" If so, CUT-THRU and stop the drain. Go through each of the steps. See what new insights come. Write them down so you don't forget. As you practice this tool, it becomes fun to spot and recoup overcare feelings and thoughts right at the start, so you ride the wave of higher care instead of getting caught in the undertow and creating a rough ride for yourself.

Intelligence is learning to increase your ratio of time spent in heart perceptions throughout a day. Until you learn the difference between mind and heart perception, you can't CUT-THRU. *It's up to you to balance yourself; no one else can do it for you.* Whatever your picture of life has been, appreciate there is a bigger picture still to be found. Appreciation opens the border between the little and big picture. In the little picture, you are stuck "knowing what you know," which closes the door to new intelligence. In the bigger picture the mind knows what you're still learning, which leaves the door open. Growth can be viewed as a video game. There is always a new level once you get good at the one you're on. *Increased intelligence means not having to repeat the same old stresses.* As you practice CUT-THRU, you are able to appreciate whatever you've been through in life and move on. This brings total security and maximum energy.

Even if you have had a very difficult life, you can still CUT-THRU. Crying over spilled milk traps you in overcare. What's done is done. The name of the game is to get your spirit into the game. It will move in with power as you practice CUT-THRU. Your spirit comes in through the heart and your heart perception regulates it. CUT-THRU helps you perceive that everyone has a heart and is doing the best they know how. Actualizing this understanding is what the world desperately needs.

Once you get to the other side of overcares, anxieties, judgments, and insecurities, you see why releasing, letting go, and forgiving, are serious acts of emotional management that yield a high ratio of return on your efforts. As you build power to flex and let go, it allows you to manage change as it occurs. In today's society, people have to cope with change at a rapid rate. Coping is like treading water. People hope they can cope rather than go under. CUT-THRU is a power tool to take you beyond coping into empowered management. It can be hard to catch the "power" in power tools because of their simple practicality. As the speed of change increases in the world, many people will look to power tools like CUT-THRU to bail them out of stress and overcare. To facilitate your use of this power tool, practice the steps while listening to the music *Speed of Balance*.[20] This music was designed to accelerate perception shifts and deep emotional release from cellular patterns and was used in the scientific studies with CUT-THRU described in Chapter 5.

Personal Responsibility

One CUT-THRU practiced can save you loads of time and energy. When people are on edge, they often say or do things they don't really mean and it can take months to heal the resentments. That's an energy and time loss. Cutting-thru at any point creates a *time shift* out of all that playout. Other people's emotional management or non-management is not your responsibility. Your own management is. You can say you reacted because someone said something to you a certain way — meaning, "I wouldn't have overcared if he'd just said it differently." That's what everyone does. It's a vicious circle and there's an emotional drain that goes with it. The mind can think your reaction is a stance of strength and power, but it shows a weakness in balance and clarity. The proof is in the lab. By practicing CUT-THRU when someone says something that causes you to react, you will change your reaction. That's real strength and power. The payoff of free energy regenerates you and gives sustaining power to balance and manage yourself if the situation comes up again. With balance, you would tell the person you want to discuss the matter with them and talk about your side of the issue, instead of going into the emotional re-action circle.

There are often episodes in life that you can't do anything about. For example, if there is an accident and your child is hurt, you have to eventually release, adapt, and move on. As you surrender in the heart to higher care, you CUT-THRU fear and hurt, then put care back into action through listening to your own common sense. As intense as a feeling of fear can be, you can still CUT-THRU. Intuitive thoughts of what to do come quickly. You are back to higher care. Then the passion to help your child can be as intensely powerful as the previous feeling of fear.

The CUT-THRU steps are powerful and profound. They are proven to bring emotional release and generate fulfillment. Results come quickly with just a little practice. It's tremendously empowering to care without becoming a victim. CUT-THRU is inner technology that allows people to become their own self-pharmacist, balancing their internal hormonal prescriptions and recouping energy lost from overcare stress. The technology creates an internal coherence between the heart (spirit), emotions, mind, and body. In the next chapter we'll explain this scientifically and look at the research studies done with CUT-THRU.

You can CUT-THRU any deficit in life and turn it into an asset with a practiced heart intelligence. You'll surprise yourself at how adept you can become at bailing out of each overcare, maybe not perfectly every time, but with an increasing ratio of efficiency, effectiveness, and ease. As you re-train your emotional and mental reactions and increase your coherence, you will re-create your life. You will reach a place where you no longer have to keep "working things out," but realize they are worked out! Productive solutions for personal problems, health care problems, environmental issues, social, economic, or political gridlocks, and new technological breakthroughs will surface as more people learn to CUT-THRU their overcares and find intuitive insight.

Chapter 5

The Science of Cᴜᴛ-Tʜʀᴜ Technology

A s I mentioned in Chapter 3, emotions and the heart were related for centuries. Sir William Harvey, who was the first to demonstrate the function of the heart and how blood circulates in the body, stated in 1628 that, *"Every affection of the mind that is attended to, either with pain or pleasure, hope or fear, is the cause of an agitation whose influence extends to the heart."* Indeed emotions can trigger a gamut of disturbances in heart rhythms, including, in extreme cases, sudden death due to ventricular fibrillation.

The idea that people can self-direct their emotions, hormones, and other aspects of their physical body is not new. Millions believe they affect their bodily functions through prayer, meditation, yoga, biofeedback, positive thinking, etc. Scientific studies increasingly support that belief. Research has shown that people who maintain positive attitudes are less likely to become ill and more likely to heal faster than those with negative attitudes.[21]

According to Deepak Chopra, M.D., one of the most widely known experts in this field, "The connection between aging and stress hormones has been strongly demonstrated, but the problem of how to control these hormones remains." Because the stress reaction can be triggered in a split second and without warning, Chopra suggests that mind-body techniques that go directly to the root of the stress response are needed.[22] As researchers discover how to create self-management tools that help people regulate their own emotional, mental, and hormonal states, this may eliminate the need for long-term dependency on drugs such as Prozac, Valium, and hormonal supplements such as estrogen.

Many people say they want to take more personal responsibility for their emotional states, and with new self-management tools this will move beyond just an idealistic concept. Responding to the need for a tool that does not require withdrawal from the everyday world or hours of intense practice which most of us haven't time for, I researched and developed the CUT-THRU technology. Working with scientists specializing in organizational behavior, psychology, cardiology, immunology, and endocrinology, the IHM research laboratory designed several studies to examine the effects of CUT-THRU. The following is a description of the theory behind the technology, the basic research, the studies, and the results.

Understanding Our Hormones

When I refer to "hormones," I am referring to any substance released by a cell which acts on another cell near or far. Hormones are chemical messengers that regulate most of the body's functions, including the way the brain processes information. This includes neurotransmitters, neuromodulators, and neurohormones, all of which are found in the brain and throughout the body. Hormones are involved in the regulation of a myriad cellular functions — digestion, fat production, muscle contraction and relaxation, the reproductive processes, growth, sexual and aggressive behaviors, and much more. Our emotions and perceptions affect our hormones, which in turn biochemically affect our emotions and perceptions, in a never-ending cycle. Researchers are still uncovering how specific hormones function in the body. A few years ago French scientists discovered that the heart secretes an important hormone, called ANF (atrial natriuretic factor) that has a balancing effect on the cardiovascular system.[23] In addition, receptors for this heart hormone have been discovered in the hypothalamus and pituitary glands in the brain which are con- sidered master regulators of the entire hormonal system.

Since the brain is the general or master regulator of the body's hormonal system, controlling our hormones has to involve the brain. The brain is "neurally" connected to virtually all parts of the body by nerves. Nerves ferry impulses from brain to body and body back to brain. All nerve cells (or neurons) in the brain receive and send messages via neurotransmitter hormones. Nerve cells communicate through synaptic transmission, where the sending cell fires an electrical signal and secretes a neurotransmitter onto the surface of a recipient neuron. The intensity of an emotional experience can affect the strength of synaptic connection. This is one reason why emotionally charged events are so easy to remember, and sometimes so hard to forget.

The Mystery of the Brain

There is a great desire in people to understand how the brain works. President Bush declared the 1990's the "Decade of the Brain" and as I was writing this chapter, the cover story of *Time* magazine (July 17, 1995) featured the brain. It was titled *"Glimpses of the Mind: What is consciousness? Memory? Emotion? Science unravels the best-kept secrets of the human brain."* The article described what scientists know about brain function in general and also raised fundamental questions scientists are asking, such as, "How is the 'self' created?" "Is memory nothing more than a few thousand brain cells firing in a particular, established pattern?" The article concludes, "In short, the brain is a hot topic, and while a complete understanding of its inner workings will be a long time coming, the surge of interest in things cerebral has already produced tantalizing results."

Everything the brain does is assumed by some scientists to be ultimately explainable in terms of specific nerve cells and neurotransmitters. However, there are anomalies that neuroscience cannot explain. For example, the brain does not store memory in one area; memory is distributed throughout the brain.[24] All brain mechanisms and hormonal releases are assumed to obey the laws of the physical universe, including electromagnetism, hydrodynamics, and quantum physics. The ability of the neuronal organization of the brain to act holistically is one of the great mysteries of neuroscience.

How is it that the brain's synaptic connections allow for the emergence of holistically distributed patterns which interweave to create the emergence of a reality within which an identity called "self" can will, imagine, feel, and think? Many scientists are convinced that quantum theory will be part of that explanation.[25] Quantum energy states obey the rules of quantum field theory which say: Particles that make up matter are inseparable from fields or wave states that give rise to or "create" the particles.[26]

The processing or computing of information in the brain may also occur in fields surrounding the neurons even before they "fire" or send bursts of information to one another.[24] IHM researchers theorize that the physical function of neurons is guided by surrounding fields which I call *causal* fields, and that throughout life, perceptions, attitudes, and memories are processed and exist dynamically within these fields. While DNA has coded within it the basic patterns for brain development, it does not determine the specific connections within neuronal structures. These form through experience. As children, our neuronal organization is flexible and changes easily in response to challenges in the environment. If children are chronically stressed, however, their ability to adapt or learn can be impaired.[27] By puberty the neurons and synapses are largely in place and "fixed." Thereafter, it takes more energy in the causal fields to reprogram the learned and fixed patterns. They become "mind-sets," which means our perceptions and responses are bound by these patterns, limiting our range of possibilities and adaptability, accelerating the aging process.

Our brain/mind constructs our experience through electrochemical fields (through mathematical rules similar to those that describe holograms). These fields set up brain circuits which can be thought of as an inner 3-dimensional TV system in which the circuitry converts the incoming signals into the sounds and words we hear and the pictures we see on the field-like "screen of the mind." But who is watching and comprehending the movie that is playing out on our inner screen and who is directing the play, making choices, and writing the script? Where does the intelligence reside which organizes the physical neurons and chemicals that allow the emergence of conscious awareness? And how is it that people whose brain and heart are clinically dead can come back to life (the near death experience) and report that they still thought, felt, and perceived while supposedly dead? These are questions that stump scientists and philosophers alike.

One possible answer that comes from brain research[24] and quantum physics points to a field domain that enfolds space and time, a dimension of intelligence that science does not yet fully understand, nor have ways to measure but which people experience. One interpretation of quantum theory mandates that physical events and subjective consciousness form a unified field system. Physicists refer to a field "vacuum" from which quantum and subatomic particles of matter are created. Fields that surround these particles, although beyond the confines of space-time, actually influence the very space-time structures they create.

The Mystery of the Heart

Research has found that the heart is far more than just a mechanical pump. The heart not only powers the body on the physical level, but IHM researchers are finding evidence that the heart, like the brain, influences information-processing capabilities. In fact, when the electrical patterns of the brain synchronize with the electrical patterns of the heart, more intuition and intelligence become available to the brain.

In the fetus, the heart starts to beat before the brain and nervous system have started to develop. A mystery of neuroscience has been the source of that heartbeat. The heart is "autorhythmic," which means it beats on its own without requiring input from the brain or nervous system. The heart beats to its own drummer. It is as yet not influenced by the brain or nervous system. Even after we are born and throughout life, the electrical energy in each heartbeat and *the frequency information contained therein* is pulsed to every cell of the body, including the brain.

Most people know that the brain generates electrical energy called brain waves — measured by electroencephalogram (EEG). The fact that the heart generates electrical energy or heart waves — measured by electrocardiogram (ECG) — which have 40-60 times more amplitude than the brain waves is not as well known.[2] Not only do the specialized pacemaker cells in the heart generate continuous output, the heart's electromagnetic field radiates to all the cells in the body and out into the space around us. The heart's electromagnetic field can even be measured several feet away from the body.[28] The frequencies that are contained in and shape this field change as our thoughts and emotions change, with emotion causing the most immediate and measurable changes in the electrical system of the heart.[2]

Scientists have found that the brain communicates to the heart, hormonal system, and immune system through the autonomic nervous system. Another important fact is that the heart also communicates to the brain through a neural link called the baroreceptor system,[6] through the hormone ANF, and through the heart's electromagnetic fields.[2] Thus, the heart informs the brain through several communication systems which directly affect perception, reaction speeds, and decision-making ability.

In examining the electromagnetic fields generated by the heart, IHM research has found that sincere "heartfelt" experiences bring about increased coherence in the heart's electromagnetic field.[2] Coherence is an aligning of the frequencies of the heart which generates an increase in power. When we are sincerely feeling love for someone, we feel it in the area of the heart, then the heart communicates the signal of love to the brain. The brain then responds by creating balanced hormonal patterns that regenerate the well-being of the entire system. When we truly love or appreciate, we seem to have endless energy, a much higher pain threshold, and more tolerance for things that would otherwise frustrate us. When we love, everything looks brighter and "our hearts come alive."

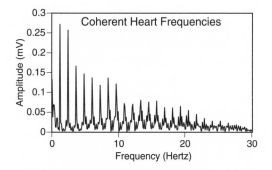

Figure 1. Coherent heart frequencies of a subject practicing CUT-THRU. This frequency domain spectrum, derived from 10 seconds of ECG (electrocardiogram) data, exhibits a harmonic series.

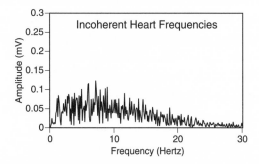

Figure 2. Incoherent heart frequencies of a subject feeling anxiety. This frequency domain spectrum, derived from 10 seconds of ECG (electrocardiogram) data, exhibits disorder and chaos in the heart's electrical system.

In our research, people report that sustaining higher heart feelings enables them to access a new dimension of expanded perception and intelligence in the causal field domain. My own experience confirms this. CUT-THRU practice allows heart, emotions, brain, and mind to entrain and become coherent, giving you the coherent power needed to access this dimension of your own intuitive intelligence.

The Power of Feeling

Studies have shown that positive feelings such as love, care, appreciation, and compassion, bring balanced and ordered internal energy flows, which in turn, result in increased coherence and harmony in the physiology of the body. Negative feelings such as anger, anxiety, and worry, on the other hand, create disorganized, incoherent, and unbalanced energy flows which eventually result in accelerated aging and physical deterioration. Sustaining balanced care throughout daily life shifts the heart's electrical frequencies into more efficient, coherent patterns which are needed to nurture the entire body.

Emotions flow through the body on an electromagnetic level much faster than information flowing along nerve pathways. When you learn to perceive from the heart, your emotions and thoughts are guided by a different energy flow than when you perceive from the mind alone. Perceptions and emotions follow the frequencies of either the mind or heart domain, wherever our energy is primarily focused. Emotions qualified or directed through the mind alone will often act like water that floods your kitchen, whereas heart-directed emotions will use that same water to quench your thirst and give substance and meaning to life. Self-empowerment is learning to call the shots on the water distribution, while non-empowerment is being a victim of random emotions. As people CUT-THRU to heart perception *before* they engage their emotions, they experience a dramatic shift in empowerment and understanding. Skill in CUT-THRU builds a *standing wave of coherence* between your heart, brain, and body. This same wave of coherence also unites spirit, emotions, and mind. The resulting intuitive awareness further penetrates into the causal field domain which exists beyond time and space. It's at this causal field level that CUT-THRU reprograms emotional and mental circuitry.

Holographic Perception Theory

Karl Pribram, M.D., one of the pioneers of modern neuroscience and author of numerous books on brain function, first introduced the holographic perception theory after years of research at Stanford University where he directed the neuroscience research center. The discovery that the brain's processing functions and memory storage are spread throughout various systems in the brain caused him to question what part of the brain integrates all the information and makes a decision. After years of research, Dr. Pribram came to the conclusion that some aspects of the brain/mind operate under holonomic or holographic principles. In holographic theory, every part contains the information of the whole at the field domain level. This theory helps explain how the brain can holistically process and store information. In these respects, the brain/mind operates in field domains wherein the interaction of frequencies gives rise to perception, thought, memory, time, space, etc.[24] Different parts of the brain select frequencies according to their specialized functions. However, if one part of the brain is damaged, then another part often takes over its function and interaction with the field domain. This has been shown to be especially true in babies and young children who have had brain damage.

In my perception, the heart's electrical domain is also a holographic information processing system. It is here that intuitive feeling enters the human system. The heart's electrical field operates like a radio receiving and transmitting station. That's why we sometimes feel the need to be alone or why it feels better to be around some people and not others. (IHM has recently developed a new method of measuring the electrical exchange of heart energy between people when they touch or are in close proximity.) The holographic heart field domain theory may also assist scientists in understanding why heart transplant patients sometimes take on the personality characteristics of their donors for a period of time.

IHM research is being called a breakthrough in health technology because it helps to clarify why positive feelings affect health and perception, along with providing scientifically tested tools such as CUT-THRU to help people achieve high performance states. Traditionally, psychology and physiology have been studied as separate disciplines. Since scientists have discovered that certain drugs affect psychological states, and that attitudes and emotions affect biochemistry, exciting new fields of research have been initiated, such as psychobiology, psychophysiology, and psychoneuroimmunology. Scientist's are discovering that as people become more emotionally coherent, the physiology of the body also becomes more coherent. Terms such as entrainment and coherence, once thought to be only metaphoric when applied to mind or emotions, have become important measurements in psychology, physiology, and physics — although their precise definitions still differ between disciplines.

Balancing the Nervous System

IHM scientists have observed three stages of increasing nervous system balance[29] from practicing CUT-THRU (or the first empowerment tool I designed called FREEZE-FRAME®).[30] When people are frustrated or stressed, their heart rhythms become irregular and disordered. Bringing your stressed thoughts and feelings to the heart and holding them there takes you to the first stage of order: *Neutral.* In neutral, the nervous system balance is increased and normal heart rhythms can be re-established. The second stage of order is called *Entrainment.* As you move from neutral into a higher heart feeling, such as love, care, compassion, or appreciation, heart rhythms become increasingly balanced and smooth. Entrainment takes place when "frequency-locking" between the heart rhythms, respiration, pulse transit time (a measure of blood pressure), and brain waves occurs. Entrainment between heart and brain activates a shift in perception and greatly increased intuitive awareness.

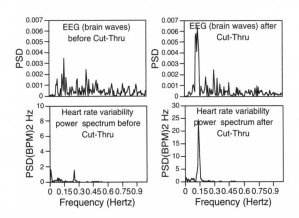

Figure 3. The graphs on the left side show the frequency analysis of the very low frequency region of the brain waves (EEG) and heart rate variability (HRV) of a subject just prior to using CUT-THRU. The graphs on the right side show that the brain waves have entrained to the heart rate variability frequency near .1 Hz. while the subject was using CUT-THRU.

As you continue to practice CUT-THRU, a third stage of balance is achieved and can be measured: *Internal*

Coherence. This is a state where both the inner dialogue and the nervous system output from brain to heart are greatly reduced, allowing you to listen to the heart with increased clarity. I call the experience of internal coherence "amplified peace." This is a state similar to the highest stage of peak performance (such as the runner's high). Business people report it as a state of "high performance."

Overcare and emotional residues prevent people from enjoying peak performance. CUT-THRU practice is designed to clean out overcares and emotional residues from the causal fields down to the cellular level. By continuing to build CUT-THRU power, amplified peace or internal coherence is sustained for longer periods. As you feel a passionate care or love for what you're doing, you intuitively perceive what to do next with a minimum of mental calculation. Blocks of intuitive information can come to you in seconds.

Hope for peace is within each individual's heart, but only through learning to listen to your heart can the potential of this hope be realized. One of the missions of the IHM laboratory is to prove what people already know intuitively — that love or true care is the forgotten factor in health. Now let's look at some of the specific research behind the development of the CUT-THRU technology.

Heart Rate Variability

The autonomic nervous system regulates many unconscious body functions, such as breathing, heart rate, hormonal balance, immune regulation, etc. The autonomic system has two main divisions, the sympathetic and parasympathetic, and the signals they generate create beat-to-beat changes in heart rate. The term describing this changing rate is heart rate variability (HRV).

Analysis of HRV is generally used to measure the balance between the sympathetic, which speeds up the heart, and the parasympathetic, which slows down the heart.[6] HRV is used by doctors as a measure of the health of the heart. The greater the heart rate variability, the healthier the heart and nervous system. Babies have extremely high heart rate variability. We lose variability as we age. Through practicing Cut-Thru, we can improve autonomic nervous system balance, which in turn improves our health and slows aging.

Donnie and the Rabbit

The IHM laboratory conducted a study on how anger affects nervous system balance. The study measured attitude traits and used a Holter machine to record the electrocardiogram (ECG) of each subject for a 24-hour period. From the ECG we can determine heart rate variability (HRV). Donnie, a volunteer construction worker for IHM, was one of the subjects. As it turned out, the day Donnie was being recorded he got angry and upset over something at work. Several people tried talking to him, pointing out all the reasons why he didn't need to be upset, but to no avail.

A rabbit had appeared at the IHM research center a few months earlier when it was only a few weeks old. Donnie liked to feed the rabbit and they had become buddies. The project manager in the lab wanted to see if Donnie would calm down if he gave him the rabbit to hold. Within minutes, Donnie's attitude, body language, and the color in his face all shifted as he started petting and caring for the rabbit. When we analyzed his ECG, we found that his heart rate variability patterns also changed when he started caring for the rabbit! The changes indicated a profound shift in his autonomic nervous system. The shift is shown in Figure 4.

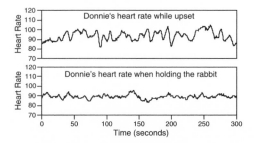

Figure 4. The top panel shows Donnie's heart rate variability patterns while he was upset. The bottom panel shows the improvement in Donnie's heart rate patterns when he started caring for the rabbit.

Several days later two of our scientists decided to reverse the experiment. They hooked up the rabbit to the ECG equipment and noticed his nervousness reflected in chaotic heart rhythms. Ten minutes later, they invited Donnie into the lab to pet and talk to the rabbit. The change in the rabbit's ECG showed that the rabbit's autonomic system balance dramatically improved as it was being cared for. Figure 5 shows the before and after HRV states of the rabbit.

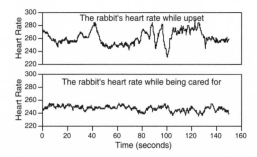

Figure 5. The top panel shows the rabbit's heart rate variability patterns while he was upset. The bottom panel shows the improvement in the rabbit's heart rate patterns when Donnie started caring for the rabbit.

The changes in both Donnie's and the rabbit's ECGs reflect changes in their autonomic nervous systems that were triggered by feeling sincere care or being cared for. Remember, it is the autonomic nervous system that regulates the hormonal and immune systems.

Similar Research Findings

The Donnie and rabbit experiments help explain the results of other experiments conducted with animals. Love has been shown to influence an animal's weight gain, emotional reactions, ability to respond to stress, and learning behaviors. Studies have shown that animals raised without love have weakened immune systems and a greater tendency to develop disease, while those exposed to love seem better able to resist disease. In one experiment, two groups of laboratory rabbits were each fed a diet high in fat. One group of rabbits was shown love; they were talked to, handled gently, and petted often. The other group of rabbits was treated routinely but not given love. The rabbits that were loved developed significantly less atherosclerosis than the rabbits treated routinely.[31]

Most people intuitively understand that attitudes affect health. But many do not realize that even five minutes of feeling true care can enhance the immune system, while five minutes of feeling anger or anxiety can suppress the immune system for hours.[19] There are a number of studies showing that care boosts the immune system. In a study at Harvard University, David McClelland found through a series of experiments that people who are more caring have higher levels of an immune antibody called IgA, which is considered to be the body's first line of defense against invading bacteria and viruses.[32] Researchers at IHM not only replicated

McClelland's work, but found two additional facts. First, people have much more power to influence and increase their IgA levels when they self-generate the feeling of care instead of having the feeling of care externally induced through watching a movie. Second, while anger is known to suppress the immune system, we found that even rehashing a previous experience that made you angry has long-term negative effects on the immune system.[33] This demonstrates why it is important to release overcares and emotional baggage. Now let's look at the CUT-THRU studies.

CUT-THRU Study #1

The hypothesis of IHM scientists was that regular practice of CUT-THRU would significantly reduce negative feelings and stress, and significantly increase positive feelings and well-being. There were 49 subjects, 15 males and 34 females. There was also a control group of 15 people who took all the tests but did not practice CUT-THRU.

None of the subjects was initially aware of the contents or purpose of the CUT-THRU technology. Prior to being taught the tool, they filled out a 118 item questionnaire regarding their mental and emotional stress levels and physiological stress symptoms. All participants then received training in CUT-THRU technology. They were also introduced to a music tape called *Speed of Balance*, which I designed to facilitate emotional balance.[20] Participants were instructed to listen to the music in conjunction with practicing the steps of CUT-THRU five days a week. They were also instructed to practice the tool whenever a situation occurred which caused them any overcare or distress.

Results (see Figure 6) showed significant increases in positive feelings of caring (18%), heart-felt emotions (love, forgiveness, acceptance, harmony and appreciation) (14%), contentment (13%), and vigor (10%). Results also showed significant decreases in feelings of stress (33%), guilt (32%), anxiety (32%), general overcare (26%), burnout (25%), depression (22%), and hostility (21%). In the control group of 15 people, no changes at all were seen in the above categories. In addition, women in the study kept daily charts of their mood swings during their menstrual cycle for one month prior to learning CUT-THRU and for two months after. The charts reported significant reductions in mood swings, depression, and fatigue associated with the menstrual period.

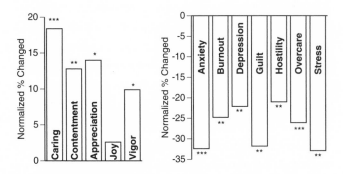

Figure 6. The bar graphs show the normalized percent increases in positive emotions and reductions in negative emotions after practicing the CUT-THRU technique for one month. (Significant p values: *p < .05, **p < .01, *** p < .001)

CUT-THRU Study #2

IHM scientists also wanted to see if regular practice of CUT-THRU would change hormonal levels of two hormones, DHEA and Cortisol. The hypothesis was that these hormones would change in a positive direction. There were 28 subjects in Study #2, 14 men and 14 women. Saliva samples were taken from all subjects prior to learning CUT-THRU and again after one month's practice. Hormonal analysis of pre and post DHEA and Cortisol levels from saliva samples was done by Dr. Elias Ilyia, director of Diagnos-Techs, Inc., a clinical and research laboratory in Seattle, Washington.

DHEA

DHEA (dehydroepiandrosterone) is the most prolific hormone in the human body and the precursor to many other hormones, including the sex hormones testosterone, estrogen, and progesterone. Although scientists are not exactly sure how DHEA works, they do know that the effects of aging become palpable when the compound's presence in the body begins to dwindle. Dr. Etienne-Emile Baulieu, a French researcher, isolated DHEA more than 30 years ago while working with testosterone and estrogen. According to Dr. Baulieu, "Increasing DHEA won't necessarily make people live longer, but it will improve the quality of life over a longer period of time and will postpone some of the unpleasant effects of aging, such as fatigue and muscle weakness."

Scientists have also linked reduced levels of DHEA with a multitude of physical disorders, including exhaustion, immune disorders, PMS, menopausal difficulties, Alzheimer's disease, obesity, and diabetes. There are also significant indications that increased DHEA levels reduce depression, anxiety, memory loss, and cardiovascular disease. Recent clinical tests at the University of California, San Diego, show that increased levels of DHEA produce increased feelings of general well-being.[34]

Dr. Norman Shealy, a well-known stress researcher and expert in DHEA explains, "DHEA is the single most important hormone in the body; it is a measure of life force." DHEA has been nicknamed the body's "fountain of youth" hormone by health enthusiasts. DHEA peaks during adolescence, then generally begins a steady decline after we reach our mid-20s. (Presently DHEA is not approved by the FDA as a hormonal supplement in the U.S. There have been no studies on the long term effects of DHEA supplements. There are also concerns about taking DHEA orally because only a small percentage is absorbed into the blood stream and much of that is broken down by the liver before the body can use it.)

DHEA Results in Study #2

In IHM Study #2, results showed an average increase of 100% in DHEA levels after one month of practice in the group of 28 subjects (see Figure 7). Some subjects tripled and even quadrupled their DHEA levels in one month. Subjects reported no dietary, exercise, or lifestyle changes during that month except for CUT-THRU practice and listening to *Speed of Balance*. Scientists have suggested that continued regular practice over time could produce even greater results.

Cortisol

Cortisol is another hormone that reacts to stress and anxiety but in the inverse direction to DHEA. Cortisol levels rise when we feel stress, especially emotional stress such as guilt, anxiety, anger, or frustration. Cortisol has been nicknamed the "stress" hormone because it is so sensitive to emotional stress. High levels of cortisol have been shown to damage brain cells and accelerate aging.[35] This is especially true if accompanied by low levels of DHEA. Cortisol is a hormonal modulator of the sympathetic nervous system, affecting cholesterol metabolism and brain processing. New research is indicating that it's not the quantity of cholesterol in the blood that causes heart disease but how much of the cholesterol is actually absorbed by the arteries. High levels of the stress hormone cortisol cause the arteries to increase absorption of cholesterol.

Cortisol Results in Study #2

In IHM Study #2, laboratory analysis showed a 23% average drop in cortisol levels after practicing CUT-THRU for one month. A further analysis was performed to test the relationship between self-reported stress and anxiety, and cortisol levels. Results showed the lower the reported anxiety and stress, the lower the cortisol, confirming the reliability of this relationship in this study.

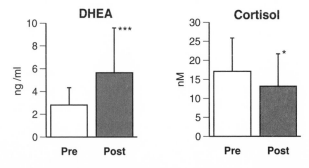

Figure 7. Shows the change in the group means of the DHEA and cortisol levels in study 2. (Significant p values: *p < .05, ***p < .001)

Study #2 is especially significant. It confirms that people have the ability to change their hormonal balance, to increase DHEA and decrease cortisol without taking drugs or supplements. This study points to the fact that we are our own self-pharmacists, and that our hormonal patterns are responsive to our changing perceptions and emotions.

The significant results from both studies came after just one month's practice of CUT-THRU by the participants. Readers interested in further information on these studies may contact IHM for research papers.

The Social Benefits of CUT-THRU

The scientific evidence on the positive effects of love and care versus the negative effects of overcare and stress on health is becoming increasingly clear. What's not at all clear to most people is how to increase love and true care. CUT-THRU is an intervention designed to increase love and true care, and transform overcare down to the cellular level. Until overcare is transformed, it will remain a personal and social predator, eating away the fabric of society, creating disorder and chaos, all in the name of care.

Social overcare always originates in a concern and sincere care, so why does it become the baseline for social ailments? The heart cares and unites; the mind overcares and separates. When emotions follow mind overcare, people are stressed. When emotions follow heart care, people are fulfilled. It's a simple equation. CUT-THRU is an intervention to approach social issues with balanced care.

Clear Perception

The key to intervention is *perception*. Why are firefighters, emergency workers, soldiers, all instructed not to panic in an emergency? Because they need to be calm to have *clear perception* and take effective action. If you need help and have two emergency workers to choose from, you would obviously pick the one who appears strong, secure, and ready to help, rather than the one who is so upset about the problem he can't see straight. A soldier is on the front line, bullets flying, bombs exploding, and he and a buddy are in a tight spot. Out of the bushes comes a shot and his buddy takes it in the leg. If he goes into overcare and panics, he'll fog with emotion, and may end up taking the next round of bullets. From the balance point of true care, he can stay calm, take control, and use his wits to get himself and his friend out of there. The endless little battles we all face in the front lines of life require the same calm, clear-headed perception to take common-sense action.

Situations that some perceive as highly stressful, others perceive as an opportunity for creativity and even fun. A teenager is competing in a basketball game and his team is losing. It's half time and his father feels that his son isn't playing his best. The parent is sweating, swearing, and stressed because his son missed a free throw. Another parent, who is less identified with his son's performance, is perceiving that both teams are having fun. That parent feels great. He is enjoying the game, not overcaring that his son also missed a free throw. He might not be ecstatic about it, but he understands it's an opportunity for his son to learn and grow.

Perception is colored by memories, attitudes, values, and ambitions. If we over-identify with ambitions and desires, we become upset when life doesn't go our way. The challenge of life is learning to make peace with situations — finding a neutral state that fosters clear perspectives. Making peace is not complacency or loss of spirit. Peace is a state of mind and heart that allows access to intuition and heightened spirit. Make peace in your heart with what *is* — then you have the power to coherently see how to change it. To be able to play the game of life well, people need to know how to do it. New intelligence is needed that will lift people to new perceptions.

When situations you don't like occur and you worry or complain, perception distorts. Life is like a mirror, reflecting back according to how we perceive. The longer people are under stress, the sharper their perception of it becomes and the more physical damage is likely to result. It's no one's fault that people haven't learned to perceive in ways that consistently benefit themselves and others. That requires new intelligence. Society has not yet had an easy step-by-step system to develop true intelligence — intellect maybe, intelligence no. The human predicament requires compassion. The mind perceives "this situation is terrible," emotions flare, and the body dutifully responds with stress. The stress response is designed to release neurochemicals that also shut down higher perceptual centers in the brain so all your energy can be available for fight or flight. If a mad dog is chasing you, you need all available energy to react fast and escape. But to solve day-to day problems, people need their higher perceptual faculties.

Increasingly, emotional stress is forcing humanity to its knees. I predict that within the next decade, out of sheer necessity, people will launch the greatest focus on emotional health and fitness the world has yet to see. Science will investigate the heart-brain communication system to discover the higher intelligence that can show people how to find real and lasting peace. No magic pill will do it.

CUT-THRU releases pent-up emotional energy and provides coherent insight so you can flow with life's changes and *move on*. It takes you from mind to heart, then heart to mind, activating the intelligence needed to adapt and address the challenges of life with a sense of security. As you practice the tool, you will understand your perceptions and feelings at a deeper level. Then validate your insights by applying them to life.

The Benefits of CUT-THRU in Business

Let's take a look at an arena where people spend much of their lives — the world of business. A key missing ingredient in business is *care*. It's clear that most people don't feel cared for at work, whether in a corporate high rise, government office, factory, or retail store. Many experts agree there is a shortage of sincerity, authenticity, and true care in most workplaces. Drained by overload and lack of care, many workers are stressed, numb, sleepwalking, and losing their effectiveness. It is my view that businesses rise and fall more due to emotional management or mismanagement than mere product success or process improvements. How a company reacts to challenges, how it treats its people, how it prepares for change, all have underlying emotional components businesses can no longer afford to ignore. An emotional virus acts like a computer virus. It can infect the system without anyone realizing it, then at a certain point the system collapses.

Executives often don't know their company has an emotional virus unless they listen well to the people. The gap between a corporation's lofty mission statement and what's actualized is frequently caused by the overcare virus. The economic system often demands that employers reengineer, restructure, downsize, or outsource work. It's *how* it's done that counts. For example, downsizing that's executed with insufficient communication or care generates fear that feels like poison in the remaining employees who are left worrying if they will be next, what extra workloads they will have to assume, and so forth. While employees are still responsible for their own reactions and stress, the statistics prove that workers need tools to build up their energy and find emotional satisfaction as they expend energy. And companies need tools to find caring and creative solutions to the challenges of improving productivity, revenue, health care, and employee relations in order to achieve their missions.

Stress Statistics in Business

A five-year study of the American work force concluded that: Many workers feel burned out by the end of the day, don't have enough time with their families, and fear they will be laid off. The study "validates what we have known in our hearts for a long time," says Burke Stinson, a spokesman for AT&T.[36] The study also found that when workers are given more freedom to take care of family concerns, productivity does not suffer. To the contrary, "employees feel like they are being treated fairly and want to give back at least what they have received."

Studies also show that upwards of 45% of career professionals in large organizations suffer from work-related emotional problems such as stress, burnout, malaise, and value conflicts.[37] Of these, 60% complain of depression, anxiety, and other troubles related to work. It's so easy to blame whoever is above you in management or blame the company for work-related problems, but it's each individual who creates their own depression or anxiety by mismanaging their internal landscape. Some people have taken jobs that are not right for them, motivated solely by money or ambition. Apathy, overcare, or fear prevent them from stepping out of roles that don't fit them. The drive for success and its criteria of money, power, and prestige parallels a less visible but increasing drive for fulfillment and meaning from work. "The tension between these two drives has unleashed a serious problem in our society," according to Washington D.C. psychiatrist Douglas LaBier.

"People used to be motivated to arrive at work early, stay late, work weekends, drag home briefcases, and dutifully check voice mail, even on vacation. But now they are asking, 'What's the point?' The perks — promotions, raises, bonuses, job security — are all but gone. The mental fatigue today is every bit as significant as the physical fatigue of the early Industrial Revolution," reported a January 1995 *Chicago Tribune* article. Indeed, in numerous surveys, stress is identified as the nation's No. 1 health issue — and job overload a major cause. Respondents to surveys use medical terms to describe themselves (e.g., "brain dead," "hemorrhaging") and their workplaces (e.g., "triage," "trauma ward").[10] It's worth noting that these views occur primarily in the U.S. In East Asia the stress approach to work persists with little questioning, while in Europe and developing countries, this type of stress is just starting to crank up.

"People at all levels in the work force report feeling stressed out, fed up, and looking for a different kind of work life," observes Dr. Robert Rosen, a psychologist who is president of Healthy Companies, a Washington-based business research and consulting organization. Rosen cites a recent Harris poll for Steelcase Inc. on "What Workers Want." Top concerns were not money, but respect, ethical managers, recognition on the job, and open communication. "This is a national trend," Rosen adds.[38]

Primarily due to downsizing, the amount of time spent on the job has grown by 158 hours a year (nearly a whole month) over the past two decades, according to Juliet Schor, a Harvard economist and the author of *The Overworked American*. At the same time, a Families and Work Institute survey found that 99% of respondents agreed with the statement, "I always try to do my job well." They just long for more personal control and care. They want to eat dinner as a family. They want to help their kids with homework. They long for purpose to their lives. They want more time, and the average worker is willing to take a 5 percent pay cut to get it, states a U.S. Department of Labor study.[36] But it's not longer work hours that prevent people from finding purpose in their lives or making time for their families. It's the emotional virus — a lack of emotional balance and self-management — that propels people to blame their problems on external factors rather than on their own responses and attitudes.

The Families and Work Institute also found that 80% of workers believe their jobs require working very hard and 65% say their jobs require working very fast.[36] Executives often think if they're not maintaining a stressful pace, someone else is, and that person's or company's work will be done faster and better. They handle stress by working even harder. Many like being under stress and even enjoy the nervous buzz. But stress becomes an addiction like any other addiction. One workaholic described his overload, "I had an inordinate need to please everyone. I tried to get eight hours of work done every morning before noon. I was always exhausted by 3 o'clock." To keep themselves going, many workaholics abuse drugs. Alcohol and cocaine are executives' drugs of choice.

It is a myth that workaholics are always more productive. What corporations are finding is that workaholics tend to make more mistakes, they're not really "present," and when they burn out, their compensation claims are twice the average worker's. The debate over sky-rocketing health care costs rarely points to unresolved emotional stress as a primary cause of rising costs. Yet compensation claims for stress-related disorders are threatening to bankrupt worker's compensation programs. Some health organizations are aware that emotional stress is a primary cause of disease, but are hesitant to publicly say so due to fear of increased claims and lawsuits against employers. They recognize that responsibility for emotional stress is individual.

Depression is a frequently misdiagnosed illness and one of the most costly to business.[39] Rates of depression have been doubling in industrial countries every ten years for decades. The depression toll is now estimated at ten percent of all employees, and a benchmark study by Massachusetts Institute of Technology estimates depression's cost to employers at $23.8 billion annually in absenteeism and lost productivity. Some companies find that employees take as much disability leave for depression as for coronary heart disease. Key indicators of employee depression are persistent sad, anxious, or empty moods, problems with sleep, eating disorders, irritability, difficulty concentrating, inappropriate feelings of guilt, thoughts of death, or suicide.

The Need for CUT-THRU Solutions

There is a formula that can reverse the stress-at-work epidemic and save money: Efficiency + Care = Power. Activating this formula would enhance productivity and improve business life for all. The CUT-THRU technology cuts-thru corporate density and malaise. As executives, managers, and workers each CUT-THRU to coherent solutions, they gain leveraged intelligence to work smarter (not necessarily harder). Individually and as teams, they perceive new ways to advance the quality of life on the job without sacrificing results. Coherent care improves wholehearted communication even with difficult bosses or co-workers. CUT-THRU unleashes that power of coherence which improves project planning and marketing, saves time, and helps people balance work responsibilities with personal life. In short, it's internal coherence that provides the personal control that workers want. When people have tools to care efficiently, the corporate culture can transform from the incoherence of an incandescent light bulb, to the power and coherence of a laser.

Here's an example of a company president using CUT-THRU in a high-stress business situation and the coherent outcome.

"I had a new product being released that was essential to providing new revenue for my growing business. I went to meet with the company who had contractually agreed to distribute the product within a short time period. When I arrived at the meeting, the president of the company and five of his key people were assembled and the mood was not good. They began by telling me that they felt that production time would take too long and that they were not going to release my product until the first of the year. Professionally and financially this was disastrous news. I felt my emotions start to boil. I tried to keep my cool on the outside but on the inside I started to react and was ready to tell them that we had a deal with a signed contract and that they were going to put this product out or else. Thoughts like 'I'm not going to let them bully me around' and 'Business is business' were racing through my mind.

"Fortunately I remembered the Cut-Thru technique. After all, it was designed to balance the emotions and if I ever needed emotional balance it was now. I focused on my heart while still listening to the distributors, looking for some feeling of peace. When I couldn't find it, I stirred my emotions in the heart like in a blender. I quickly began to feel a release. I asked myself what a fair heart solution for both sides might be. Instead of reacting, I had a clear perception of a simple solution that could speed up production time and shared it with the group of executives. Some began to discount my suggestion and others began to acknowledge its potential. Again, I started to emotionally react, but instead I went deeper in the heart and kept working with the Cut-Thru technique. I offered other reasons why I felt it was best to go ahead with my plan. Slowly the feel of the meeting began to shift. Soon they were talking among themselves and coming up with creative solutions to this timing problem. Their excitement increased and they began to offer me the use of their vendors who owed them favors and even offered to pay for the packaging design. I was sincerely amazed. I left the meeting with a sense that they had a new excitement about my product and that I had earned another important level of respect from them. When I got to my car, I sat for a moment and reflected on how things would have come out if I had not stopped and used the Cut-Thru technique. I was able to clearly see that forcing the issue would have created more resistance and resentment from them instead of cooperation. By balancing my emotions with Cut-Thru, I was able to maintain poise and clarity and it opened the others up to new ideas. The outcome was exactly what I needed for my business."

As this president realized, the meeting could have ended in gridlock if he hadn't CUT-THRU to a new solution that worked for both sides. Much of the increased stress in business is due to lack of quality communication. Yet "quality" is a major goal and buzzword in business. Everyone wants more quality in management, products, and services. Quality has "care" built into it. Customers are demanding it. It's not just quality products and services that people want, it's also quality care and respect for their needs. When businesses know how to make intelligent care a work ethic, they will see total quality increase, health care costs decline, and regain the loyalty they need from employees and customers alike.

Care is a powerful, creative motivator. As I said earlier, feelings of care are to the human system as lubricating oil is to an automotive system. Care improves hormonal balance, enabling people to operate creatively, with intuitive clarity, and improved decision-making. When care is the motivating factor, the resulting emotional balance allows you to see the whole picture at once. Your next frames of perception will then offer rewarding solutions.

Caregiving Professions

This is a book on care, so I'd like to give some care to a special group, the caregivers themselves. These are people who have chosen careers of service to those in need. The world would be in a sorry state if we didn't have these men and women, whether paid workers or volunteers dedicated to caring for others. Try being in a hospital without nurses to look after your needs. Try walking in a hospital worker's shoes for a week to see what is really behind being a caregiver. These are people who daily face the effects of trauma and violence, the ravages of AIDS, heart disease, and cancer, the effects of addiction and self-abuse. Caregivers assist the mentally, emotionally, and physically wounded. It's a difficult job, but people in caregiving professions can CUT-THRU and be more balanced and effective in all they do.

Brian was entering his first year of medical school. His exuberance to study and understand the human system was enormous. Ever since he was a young child he always cared and wanted to help people feel better. Seeing him eight years later, I gazed in compassion, sincerely wondering what had happened to him. Yes, he finished medical school and had been Dr. Brian Jamison, M.D., for four years. I thought to myself, caregivers seem to have so much responsibility to care, that they become burdened and slowly the spirit of caring they started with vanishes.

A 1992 study published in the *Annals of Emergency Medicine* concluded that "a disproportionate number of emergency physicians report high levels of stress and depression." Dr. Murray Rosenthal, a psychiatrist who started a burnout "hot line," often has clients who seem to be "making it" professionally, but whose spouses complain of isolation and abandonment.[40] "Somewhere along the way, they forgot to smell the roses and lost the meaning of life," says Rosenthal. "It isn't hard work that kills you," he adds, "It's when you're pouring out energy and feeling that it just doesn't matter. It's the helplessness, the futility that burns you out. The patterns don't change, unless you change what's going on inside."

A common factor found in the rising number of malpractice insurance claims is communication problems between doctor and patient. In a study published in the April 1993 issue of *Medical Care,* more than a third of physicians reported experiencing frustration in 25% of patient visits. When physicians are dissatisfied with a patient session, they may feel sad, overwhelmed, angry, and rejected, affecting their next patient session. The study found that physicians usually attributed communication problems to the patient rather than to their own limitations.

When caregivers depersonalize patients too much and cut off their heart feelings, emotional exhaustion (an index of burnout) sets in. Psychiatrists and social workers are most susceptible. Emotional exhaustion and perceptions of uncontrollability eventuate in depression. Surveys of psychiatrists, psychologists, and social workers conclude that although rewarding, these professions are often demanding, lonely, and frustrating, with feelings of ineffectiveness.

Caregiving is a career in which people easily fall prey to overcare and burnout. It's understandable why caregivers get disappointed, exhausted, and eventually dispirited. Numerous studies of nurses reveal that nurses are burdened due to heavy workloads, lack of control, and lack of appreciation. A shortage of nurses, a large turnover, along with fewer people entering the nursing profession, create feelings of dismay. Hospital politics bring additional anxiety that wears down the caregiver and gives rise to judgments of the hospital or employing organization that further shut off the heart.

Yet it is still a matter of perception. There are doctors, psychologists, nurses, and social workers who are able to stay emotionally balanced and release overcare. This is not to say they don't have to deal with other people's unrealistic expectations and other work-related problems. However, a study of 115 registered and practical nurses using the Maslach Burnout Inventory showed that it's **a sense of personal control** over the things that happen in life and in the work environment that protects nurses from emotional exhaustion, depersonalization, and lack of personal accomplishment.[41]

It's when overcare stacks from mole hills into mountains that caregivers lose the vision of why they chose caring as their life's work. *"I feel like in six years I've probably aged twenty or thirty years, and I probably have seen more in six years, as far as human nature and the basics of human life, than most people will ever see in a lifetime,"* one nurse lamented. Researcher Carol Montgomery responded, *"This exposure could be experienced as gaining philosophical wisdom, or simply as wearing down of the spirit."* It can go either way, depending on the inner balance of the caregiving professional.

A nurse learned her mother had cancer that had spread to the lungs. Her mother had already had chemotherapy for breast cancer five years before and the family had hoped it was over. In spite of all the nurse's experience with cancer patients, she found herself deeply upset about her mother. She had used CUT-THRU easily with other overcares, but this one took more effort.

"I kept using CUT-THRU, going through the steps, and finally was able to manage my emotions enough to find peace. That changed everything. I was able to help my mother find her peace. She needed to emotionally know I was okay so she didn't have to support me emotionally and keep a brave face. Now she's using CUT-THRU, especially after chemotherapy when the side effects are so bad. She feels she now has something to do with all the fear and helpless feelings. She's doing a terrific job keeping herself emotionally balanced. The tumor in her lung had been enlarging but now it's going down. With Cut-Thru, I've been able to have fun with my mother as we focus on living as opposed to focusing on death."

Overcare occurs when the head takes over. It's the head that worries, fears, and has expectations of others, even of humanity, or of God. When expectations are not met, caregivers feel disappointed, drained, and eventually dispirited. However, Montgomery's study of nurses demonstrated that it isn't caring that leads to burnout, but rather a lack of caring when the heart shuts down. It's important to reiterate the conclusion of her study, "Caring itself allows nurses to access a very important source of energy and renewal."

Practicing Cut-Thru can assist the caregiver in finding a balanced perspective, improving communication, and taking control even amidst difficult circumstances. With Cut-Thru, nurses, doctors, and social workers can make the choice to care in the heart for patients and for those they know will never recover. The caring itself will be the gift they give, even when they cannot give healing. Finding the flow through the heart again is what makes it all worthwhile.

Other Caregivers

Day-to-day life in a classroom can be extremely stressful for teachers. Educators who care for children report that the increased emotional needs of students today are a major source of their stress. Overcare can easily take over. One-third to one-half of all new teachers quit within the first three years largely out of frustration over curriculum requirements and too many discipline problems, according to statistics.[42]

By learning to Cut-Thru to true care again, teaching can be a very fulfilling job. Here's an account from a teacher who transformed his teaching experience through CUT-THRU technology.

"Sometimes my junior high students would deliberately try to sabotage my writing lessons by pretending ignorance of the instructions or complaining that they had no idea where to begin. In the case of one boy, we both knew he was playing games with the lesson. He wanted to win the battle of wills and didn't care about consequences. I tried story idea starters, I tried coaxing him, I tried this and I tried that. Bad grades, calls to the parent, extra homework, or office detention were all ineffective. Nothing worked and my care was turning into frustration as my enthusiasm was being drained.

"Something was missing in my approach. From my bag of tricks learned through ten years of teaching, I was at a total loss as to what to do. I knew my frustration was carrying over to my other classes and to after work hours at home. I had learned the CUT-THRU tool so I decided to try it out during my prep period. I observed my inner weather as partly cloudy. I went to my heart and floated as if I was floating on my surfboard which I used to do in my junior high years. Relax and let go, I told myself. Just feel the good feeling. After a minute or so, I really did feel a sense of peace. Holding to the peace, I refocused on the defiant boy and went to the fair heart to reflect clearly. Here I am, trying to inspire and motivate him, and totally failing. What is going on in his world? What is motivating him to act out and not cooperate? I began to see how this boy must have problems with adults and authority to such extent that his primary motivation is to recover some self-esteem which has been lost or crushed. At least he is determined to win some battles at school whereas perhaps at home he feels like a constant loser. These realizations set me free from my frustration. At least now I had an understanding.

"Just by taking this seven-minute break from the action and reaction mentality that I was previously operating from, CUT-THRU allowed me to see into this boy's world much more deeply than before. Of course! He needs some form of expression to give him some confidence and sense of his own authority. It was pretty obvious, now that I realized it, but sometimes as a teacher with all the responsibilities, it's hard to see a student's world in the short time spans we have with them. Another insight! I initiated a classroom discussion theme about laws and rules and what role they play in our society. We discussed how teenagers are defining their own individuality with their own opinions and that part of the process is questioning authority, examining what is right, what is fair and unfair. Without this growing up process, they would not become responsible adults with their own discrimination. In the discussions, the boy came alive as I had never seen before. Some of his positions and opinions were extreme and drew critical comments from other students. But I pointed out that there was some truth in his comments because some adults are heavy-handed and don't really understand adolescents. The fact that he expressed his strong feelings and that I understood and even backed him to some degree was a turning point. It represented a place for us to begin working together for the first time. While his skills were not exemplary nor was his classroom demeanor, he began trying some writing activities because he had been understood, maybe for the first time. It was gratifying to see this shift in him and to find myself free from the previous turmoil. CUT-THRU really cut-thru this issue for me."

The issue of caregiving is not just for people in caregiving careers, but touches us all. Many of society's problems, from juvenile crime to illiteracy, reflect inadequate care of our youth. While young working parents search for reliable child care, millions of other workers are facing elder care issues. By the early 21st century there will be more people 65 or older than under 18. Former first lady Rosalynn Carter believes America is in the midst of "a caregiving crisis." Medical science has made such progress that people survive serious trauma, heart attacks, and accidents and then sometimes have to be cared for the rest of their lives. Surveys show one-fifth of the nation's workers will become caregivers in the next several years.

Along with Susan K. Golant, Rosalynn Carter has written a book, *Helping Yourself Help Others: A Book for Caregivers*. "For anyone who has ever helped a family member or a friend in the throes of a lengthy or terminal illness, nothing is quite as disheartening or stressful as the lonely despair of not knowing where or to whom to turn for support," says Carter. "Some find the task so daunting, they themselves become sufferers, experiencing emotional and physical fatigue, family conflicts, social isolation, and feelings of anger, resentment, hopelessness, anxiety, and grief. Guilt is a frequent emotion for people who are dealing with the physically and mentally dependent," adds Carter.

Sincere Love and Care Can Heal

In the research studies on CUT-THRU described in Chapter 5, it is highly significant that feelings of guilt were reduced by an average of 32% as feelings of love and care increased. In "The Subtle Energy of Love," Judith Green, Ph.D. and Robert Shellenberger, Ph.D., summarize the research on the positive effects of love on health.[43] The authors quote Martin Heidegger, the famous German phenomenologist who stated, "the essence of love is caring." They say, "He seems to be accurate. 'Caring' is a common theme in all meanings of love and another way of describing love is by the degree of caring involved in the particular situation." Two important studies back this up, although there are many published studies that show the critical importance of emotional support in health and healing. In a five-year study of angina pectoris (heart spasms) among 10,000 men, published in the *American Journal of Medicine*, blood cholesterol, ECG, blood pressure and anxiety, and family and psychosocial problems all were measured. The family problems questionnaire included the question, "Does your wife show you her love?" Response to this question turned out to be the best predictor of the development of angina. The study concluded that "the wife's love and support is an important balancing factor, which apparently reduces the risk of angina pectoris even in the presence of high risk factors." In another study, published in *Psychosomatic Medicine*, the quality of marital relationship and immune functioning were compared in 473 women. The study found that "the more supportive the marital relationship, the more competent the immune system."

Have you ever cared for someone and seen the sparkle and hope come back into their eyes? Or perhaps you've watched them make more effective and efficient choices with their lives. Think of a time when a teacher, counselor, or mentor provided care and encouragement for your development. That's what motivated you to learn something new or stretch yourself past your limitations. The reason it stands out in your memory is the **care** they showed you.

Millions of unrecognized people have been on the giving side of the care equation. They are firemen, missionaries, volunteers who work in soup kitchens, on rescue squads, at homeless shelters, in huts teaching children, ministering to the sick, and countless others. The world is a service-oriented and caring place. In essence, many people are caregivers and need to be. Although accurate statistics on the number of homeless are impossible to formulate, the most widely cited statistic is that approximately 500,000-600,000 homeless people in the U.S. can be found in shelters, eating at soup kitchens, or congregating on the street at any one time. In 1994, nearly 25 million meals were served at soup kitchens and shelters in the U.S. Whether it's on the streets, in Africa, or in a schoolroom, true care — without the overcare — can make a difference. The world can use all the care that it can get. Care is what makes life worthwhile. CUT-THRU can start to put the world of any caregiver back into the right perspective. True care, without all the overcare, can make caregiving an opportunity for renewal of spirit rather than hopeless victimization. It's our choice.

Political Care

In the political arena we find compounded stress. Numerous politicians are stressed and have lost contact with the heart of care amidst political interactions.

Governments are gridlocked with social, health, environmental, and money deficit issues. Politicians perceiving primarily from the head develop self-centered ambitions, forgetting that care, cooperation, and co-creation would produce more harmony, balance, and success for their constituents and their country.

A majority of politicians are lawyers and business people who have had to confront many political, judicial, and ethical issues to get elected. The political system fosters cut-throat debates with little heart. In his book, *The Lost Lawyer: Failing Ideals of the Legal Profession,* Yale University law professor Anthony T. Kronman argues that "the work itself is so draining and so exhausting that it leaves little emotional and intellectual reserve behind." Attorneys suffer from depression and substance abuse at twice the national average.[44] Ambition over-drive, fatigue, and the frustration of working in government eventually catch up with most politicians. "I got the impression of drowning very quickly after getting there," said one elected official. "I was doing Band-Aid treatment . . . there was a tremendous personal toll."

Self-centered ambitions and infighting over every issue, whether it's the national debt, crime, health care, the environment, or foreign policy, are causing respect for government to plummet. Governmental stalemate demonstrates that people care (or overcare) more for issues, ideals, and money than they do for each other. Society is learning these lessons the hard way. A lack of care and respect for each other as human beings is causing our ecological and political systems to decay. Nevertheless, a paradigm shift is underway. A paradigm shift is a fundamental change in the way masses of people perceive life. A large number of people will soon perceive and affirm that true care is what's missing in the social institutions that formulate our lives. If and when the governments of the world begin to act with true care for all people, they will help bring the dream of a harmonious world into reality.

Imagine no homeless people. No disputes that are solved by wars. No countries with a majority of people starving. Sincere care is the active perception that can find solutions that will bring these dreams into actuality. Separation and impasses are man-made fences. There is a lot of head confusion, along with a lot to take care of, and politicians also need compassion for their efforts. While those who seek political positions often are motivated by power and wealth rather than the good of the whole, it's not solely their fault that governments and the world are in the state they are. Most people would find it very difficult walking in their shoes, dealing with complex political and social issues every day. Politicians reflect the general state of confusion of those they are supposed to be leading. As people wake up to this fact and become more responsible, they will elect leaders who reflect responsibility and integrity. Then some of the fences can fall and the puzzle of how to run the world would become simpler to solve.

Currently, there's a whole range of issues creating gridlock within the U.S. government that are crying out for balance, insight, and fairness. Yet emotions race out of control and over-identification clouds assessment in making decisions which have deep and long-lasting consequences. For example, a strong national and political tide has turned against entitlement programs in the effort to balance the budget. The original intention of entitlement was to help the young, the old, and those who could not care for themselves. For the unemployed, welfare was supposed to provide short term assistance until people could get back on their feet. The unintended consequence of entitlements has been to create a huge culture of dependency. Government mismanagement, crime, and a culture of poverty assail many people dependent on handouts. It is not a productive outcome nor a pleasant way to live. The system does need redesign.

Some angrily stereotype a whole sub-culture of entitlement recipients as lazy, spoiled, and violent. Others blame society for historic injustices that have created and concretized a lower class marked by discrimination and poverty. Both positions reinforce a victimization stance — somebody else is responsible for this mess so let them fix it. Neither approach offers hope or empowerment.

Though most agree that something needs to be changed, true dialogue and the application of the fair heart has been buried behind hysterical charges and counter charges. No doubt the debate (which continues as of this writing) will produce some kind of change. But there is also no doubt that great amounts of bickering, name calling, confusion, and aspersions will be cast before the debate is over. Much time and creative energy is squandered on unbalanced emotional debate. If the players in the political process used the CUT-THRU tool, politicians in government would find responsible and more complete solutions instead of shape-shifting one area only to cause worse problems in other areas. With some emotional management and intuitive insight, our representatives could accomplish far more, far more quickly, and offer a positive role model to the rest of the nation of how we can responsibly and fairly deal with complex issues. Emotionally volatile mind-sets prevent and block the real sense of nationhood — the heart connection of many different kinds of people who share love, honor, and hope for their country.

Ideals and Issues

With global warming, oil spills, species becoming extinct, and smog hanging over numerous cities, many are concerned about the ecology of our planet. The easy access to guns, the proliferation of sophisticated weapons, and the increase in crime have spawned a raging debate on gun control versus the rights of the individual to own a gun. Millions of unwanted pregnancies and impoverished children keep the issue of abortion rights heated as "right to lifers" fight to legislate their beliefs over women's "right to choose" abortion. Extremists have shot and murdered doctors and patients at abortion clinics. It's important to care and get involved in social concerns. But allowing care to turn into overcare in the name of a cause or an ideal and then turn into no care for some, averts the goodwill intention and often results in tragedy. The planet is toxic with stress because of a lack of true care and distortions from the emotional virus of overcare. The negative energy seriously affects the planetary balance. The world is a highly complex, interdependent system, so distortions in human consciousness affect the rhythms of nature. People are on the verge of realizing that their own negative thoughts and feelings of anger add to global toxicity. Societies will soon perceive that the real need is to clean up one's own inner ecology before launching concentrated efforts to change the outer effects. Once they do, they will intuit more efficient directions to balance the outer ecology. As people CUT-THRU to true care, common-sense resolutions for governmental and environmental issues will follow.

Sports

Many people enjoy sports to ease the strain of day-to-day living. Whether you play sports or just watch, you probably look forward to the fun, release, and social interaction it provides. Many consider sports events the highlights of their lives. But for others, watching or playing sports can be stressful.

Anxiety over a game not turning out as you want can keep you up all night and ruin the next day. Whole cities get depressed over a Super Bowl loss. Soccer fans riot and trample spectators when their team loses. Golf stress is considered a cause of death in Japan. A *Wall Street Journal* article recently reported that doctors estimate 5,000 golfers die on fairways each year because of the stressful nature of golf in Japan.[45] The article concluded that the high death rate probably stems from the combination of alcohol, sleep deprivation, and continued stressful competitive pressures on the course.

Take golf or any sport you like to play. It starts out fun, but once the novelty of learning wears off and you start judging yourself or others for not playing better, frustration and overcare set in, and the fun of the sport is gone. Involvement with sports begins with true care and fun for yourself and your team. Once your thoughts and emotions get amped up about a play, a referee call, that ball that was missed, etc., this starts a mind/solar plexus combination of negative feelings that bleed energy. Good sportsmanship and team effort are part of why people find sports so appealing. Remember it's how you play the game that counts, not whether you win or lose. Add ambition and the wrong kind of competition to sportsmanship and team effort, and you've just ruined a good game for your teammates and yourself. So don't overlook the benefits of CUT-THRU on the playing field, and don't forget to use it.

A tennis player told me this story:

"One of my biggest challenges in sports is performance anxiety. I put a lot of mental and emotional pressure on myself. Because I am blessed with a sound stroke and power, I win a lot of matches. But with my competitive drive, I'm sometimes too eager to return a shot. Performance suffers. During the heat of a match, mistakes aggravate me and I lose my sense of timing. Pros tell me not to play tense but to relax so that my footwork and body mechanics coordinate better. I've known this but was not successful at it until I learned CUT-THRU. What the tool enabled me to do was keep my inner composure. I practice in between serves or after a scored point. Just knowing how to release overcare and move energy through my heart gives me confidence in my ability. I've learned to CUT-THRU anxiety in a way no coach was able to teach me."

In professional sports, intense focus is placed on winning, money, and glory. Nearly all coaches define themselves solely on their won-loss record, leaving them especially vulnerable to overcare stress. They tend to be at high risk for heart disease, and many quit due to stress. Bill Walsh, former coach of the San Francisco 49ers, gave up professional coaching, citing, in part, the pressure. "It almost consumes you," said Walsh, who retired after leading San Francisco to three of the last eight Super Bowl championships.[46] "There were years when I was so enmeshed in my work that I lost energy — lost the will to handle the job." The performance demands by owners, fans, and the press are unreal, especially with high-priced player contracts and franchises.

In high school and college sports, athletic burnout has become a serious problem. Psychologists say society's increasing pressure to win, to be Number 1, is one of the most significant factors. Gone are the days when just making the varsity was enough. "Kids are not willing to be bench players anymore," says Lance Eddy, who has coached high school sports for 25 years.[47] "If they're not a star, they don't want to play. Just being a member of a team is not a big thing anymore." Sports is supposed to build character, teach self-sacrifice, discipline, and fair play. However, the "win at any cost" attitude has become so significant that the potential positive benefits of sports are overwhelmed.

Among female athletes, three medical disorders make up what experts now define as the female-athlete triad — increasing obsession with thinness, athletic burnout, depression (and for some, a suicide attempt). Anorexia and bulimia — the binge-purge eating syndrome — are epidemic, according to the American College of Sports Medicine. Eating disorders, along with intense training, low body fat, and stress, can lead to a variety of problems including irritability, absence of menstruation, kidney damage, irregular heartbeat, and cardiac arrest. Self-worth is defined in terms of length or frequency of exercise. Injuries, particularly small, nagging ones, can indicate mounting unhappiness and worries. To many observers, sports trends emulate life, and the sports burnout syndrome is following society's lead.

With CUT-THRU, people can neutralize sports overcares on the spot and perform their best while they play. Synchronicity between heart and brain and internal coherence create a physiological state of peak performance that allows you increased perception and awareness of the plays at hand. CUT-THRU empowers you to "be present" in the moment or "in the zone" as you play. When you watch or play a sport, practice CUT-THRU right along with it, and you'll be able to stay in touch with the pleasure of the game, focus your care and passion, have fun, and reap the rewards.

Business, caregiving, politics, sports, are all social arenas in deep need of a renewal of care. The social implications of lack of care impact us all. Nevertheless, social change starts with you. CUT-THRU is a cure for social ailments as individuals apply the technology. As each heart transforms, it creates a standing wave of heart power and coherence that helps people around you, society, and the world. With 5.5 billion people on the earth, it will take a powerful coherent force to shift the world to true care. Once enough people find balance and coherence, a global paradigm shift can happen quickly. As the laws of quantum physics state, time and events can change quickly to offer a new, more hopeful and intelligent reality. However much we might want to have someone else do it for us, a more caring world starts with a more caring relationship with yourself. You have to find peace in your own heart before you will have peace in the world.

Chapter 7

The Benefits of CUT-THRU in All Relationships

I f the first and most important relationship to care for is the relationship with one's own self, why is self-care so difficult for most people? One reason is that we are with ourselves all the time! Except when we are in deep sleep, we are continuously experiencing perceptions, feelings, thoughts, and reactions. These internal processes consume a lot of energy. People often try to take care of self by looking for some type of stimulation to renew their energy and feel more of the textures of life. Then come the experts who tell us that taking care of health means restricting pleasures we enjoy.

For physical care, we are told to exercise more, eliminate fatty foods, don't smoke, don't drink, don't eat much red meat, don't eat salt, don't eat too much sugar, read food labels — the list seems endless. For many it's just too much enjoyment to give up. As a result, consumption of fatty foods is on the increase despite all the warnings. Another reason self-care is difficult is that the prescriptions are often confusing. For years, experts advised us to eat margarine, not butter. Now they say margarine is just as bad as butter. For years people were told that alcohol is bad for your heart. Now studies show that drinking up to two glasses of wine per day is good for your heart. Even with all the do's and don'ts, between two-thirds and one-half of all heart disease is not caused by the known physical risk factors of high cholesterol, smoking, or sedentary life style.[48] People finally have to learn tools for self-maintenance in caring for health.

When it comes to emotional self-care, most people don't know where to begin. Many don't think that caring about their emotions is that important. We're taught in school to manage emotional outbursts, but the emotional bleeds go on inside that we don't suspect. If you had a computer readout at any given time, and could see how much your mind chews on emotional issues throughout the day, you would see the lack of self-care. Once your emotional energy gets leaked away, it leads to nerve energy drain. Your body then runs on nervous energy. That cuts off positive feelings and life turns into cardboard living. Millions live this way in a society that has become obsessed with looking good while feeling bad.

It takes emotional buoyancy to experience a continuity of rich textures in life. People or situations can still throw you off, but when your emotional buoyancy is up it's easier to deflect or be above the situations. It's not like you're on a ladder looking down. Buoyancy fills your emotional accumulators with energy so situations feel different. Some try to mend emotional drains with the mind, but the more they try, the more the mind tends to justify the bleed-off, which leads to running on nerve energy again. Emotional self-care goes past being even-tempered or presenting a good "storefront" appearance. You can be mild tempered but full of emotional judgments which actually take energy to sustain and finally leave you feeling dried up.

A tremendous amount of energy in the world is also bled off by self-judgments, so much in fact that people wouldn't believe how much. One of the easiest justifications for emotionally judging oneself is all the "poor me's" that get stacked. Consistent energy assignments to self-judgments, vanity identities, and performance anxiety are like thieves in the night stealing away your energy. A constant standing wave of energy is needed just to sustain insecurity perceptions. Tucking your emotional energy leaks is self-care and you can immediately see the power saved. Until you build up your emotional bank account, you can't make needed attitude adjustments. When you're running on nerve energy, you have no power to change.

How many times have you heard someone say, "Well, I don't care about myself, I just care about my family, job, church, social cause, etc.?" This may sound noble, but it's common sense that we can only give what we have. Self-care is like money in the bank — money representing the energy you have to give. If your account is empty, you can't adequately respond to your family's needs nor buy food to feed the homeless. Self-care has to be first.

A lack of self-care in society is reflected in high rates of self-abuse and abuse of others. Alcohol and drug abuse, elder abuse, child abuse, spousal abuse, all have their root cause in a lack of emotional self-care. Each year billions are spent on prescription drugs for emotional ailments, such as anxiety and depression, with billions more spent on drugs to combat eating disorders, hypertension, and diseases that result from (or are made worse by) a deficiency of emotional self-care. Taking an anti-depressant or other drug does not deal with the underlying problem.

Multitudes of people who did not feel cared for as a child or even as an adult believe they are unworthy. Their inner dialogue tells them they don't deserve care or that no one cares. As lack of self-worth conditions the mind, fear and worry can consume your reality. The mind projects images of worst possible scenarios. If a loved one is late coming home, the mind can conjure up pictures of accidents or deceit, then the emotions react in fear, the heart pounds, the body has to work harder.

When people feel they've failed at a relationship, they also tend to judge themselves harshly and feel guilty. They erroneously think that through self-beating, mistakes will be resolved or at least not repeated. Lingering in regret is a serious overcare drain. Once you CUT-THRU to increased perception, you are able to sincerely forgive yourself and others and free yourself from self-negating emotional patterns. Just as children are incredibly receptive to positive perspectives when offered with sincerity and common sense, so, too, is the adult mind when it learns to listen to its own heart intelligence with sincerity and common sense.

If you don't like yourself, try looking at yourself objectively, as though you were somebody else. Can you find a way to have compassion for this person's situation in life? If you can't, care enough to practice CUT-THRU, then answer this question. It's obvious that self-care is required to find fulfillment in life. Many people try to care for themselves by getting professional help or by following the latest therapeutic or self-help prescriptions. These efforts can help, but often do not bring complete relief. While the help of a professional can be critically important in many situations, CUT-THRU helps you discover the real therapist inside yourself, your own heart intelligence. In fact, the most effective professional therapists are those who help you listen to and understand your own heart. While this technology can be viewed as a new therapeutic model, it's designed to be self-therapeutic, giving you the power to understand and transform yourself.

Creating a Self-Care Agenda

What areas of your life need more self-care? You finally have to slow down and ask that question of your heart. Use CUT-THRU to find emotional balance and direction regarding what you eat, how much to exercise, whom to go to for advice or support, and attitudes you need to change to be fulfilled. It's a productive way to regenerate your energy supply to enjoy the buoyancy and enjoyment that life has to offer. It's math, like one plus one equals two — common sense in action. From the position of CUT-THRU care, you can take care of yourself mentally, emotionally, and physically.

Make a list of things about yourself that you care about as well as a list of people, places, things, issues, and events you care about. Put a plus next to the items that you enjoy and don't cause stress. Put a minus next to the ones that cause you some stress and are draining. These are the ones where you have overcare. For example, let's say you care about your weight, your appearance, your house, your work, your child, your cats, and your elderly father. Your weight and your elderly father have a lot of stress attached to your care. You love food, that's a plus. But you are moderately overweight. You are a yo-yo dieter which takes a lot of energy. That's a minus. You love your elderly father and are glad to care for him on one level. That's a plus. However, you are concerned about his memory loss, that he might fall and hurt himself, and worried that his needs will become more than you can handle. You're already stretched juggling work, child, and household. You know that worrying about your father causes you to eat more junk food than you should. If you CUT-THRU and find balanced care in relation to your father, you can see how to transform the overcare deficits. Through emotional balance, you access new insights on how to not worry, yet take caring action.

Pick one overcare from the list you just made. Read the sample assets/deficits sheet on the next page, then create a similar sheet for yourself. Describe the situation and what you think you should do about it. Now write down all the care assets, then write the overcare deficits next to each asset. Practice CUT-THRU until you gain a new insight. You will create a perception shift and a solution. (See the following sample page of how one person used the assets/deficits sheet to solve a problem that had been worrying her for weeks.) Even if your insight seems too simple, you'll know it's intuition if it brings you a feeling of hope or release. Write your conclusion and follow through with it. Only by acting on intuitive intelligence can you validate its reality. Do the same with all the other overcares on your list. As you transform your overcare deficits into new assets, you will create an overall shift in your life. By building a continuity of intuitive intelligence, you can transform all deficits into assets.

When you validate your insights, you accrue powerful leverage to CUT-THRU the next overcare. Take inventory on issues that are causing you energy drains and use CUT-THRU with each one to build personal power. Each overcare can be like a video game, with the obstacles becoming fun challenges you take on. Through the heart comes a solution and a mission accomplished.

Adult/Adult Relationships

When I reflect on life's richest or most painful moments and the overcares that ensued from them, they

CUT-THRU® ASSETS / DEFICITS SHEET

1. Fill out Assets column.
2. Fill out Deficits column.
3. With heart intelligence, CUT-THRU, and write down new perceptions/solutions in the CUT-THRU column, and it becomes a new asset.

DESCRIBE THE SITUATION, AND WHAT YOU ARE PROPOSING TO DO ABOUT IT:

Too much housework now that I'm working full-time.
Decision: Shall I hire a cleaning service?

Assets	Deficits	➡	CUT-THRU Creatively
More time for myself, more quality family time	— None —	➡	Complete asset!
Relieves stress of nagging my husband and kids to help.	Kids could miss out on the value of helping the family.	➡	Save out several jobs for the kids to keep as their weekly "chores."
A cleaning service can probably clean _better_ than I can!	Depends on who does it – I've heard stories of poor quality where you end up cleaning up after them.	➡	Take the time to really communicate the quality I expect. Give feedback when I see a need for improvement.
Fewer chores mean less pressure on my bad knee	Knee could stiffen up if all I do is sit at my desk.	➡	Spend some of my new-found time getting quality exercise.
	Security of valuables – heard stories of theft by cleaning people.	➡	Put more items in safe deposit box. Store silver at Aunt Sally's place.
	Will cost MONEY – so, less money to spend on other things.	➡	True. But the assets above make me feel like the expense will be worth it.

CONCLUSION: Hire the cleaning service for at least the "3-month trial offer." Call them tomorrow!!

usually involved other people. Have you ever had a good friend and then noticed the closeness just wasn't there any longer? Did you ask yourself, "Was I not caring enough?" or "Why didn't she care more?" Head processors can stack into judgments, frustration, and blame, and soon you are mad at each other and wondering what happened. I think most would agree that friendship is worth nurturing.

Today, one-quarter of American households consist of a single person. This is unprecedented in our nation's history. Loneliness is a major problem. James J. Lynch, author of *The Broken Heart: The Medical Consequences of Loneliness*, states: "Almost every segment of our society seems to be deeply afflicted by one of the major diseases of our age — human loneliness. Loneliness is not only pushing our culture to the breaking point, but is also pushing our physical health to the breaking point, and indeed has in many cases already pushed the human heart beyond the breaking point."[49] Social isolation contributes not only to loneliness but depression, and depression is also one of the highest risk factors for heart disease. Research shows that emotional support (but not dependency) on the other hand, relaxes the heart, lowers blood pressure, and has a beneficial effect on the brain.[13]

Caring communication boosts understanding, emotional support, and loyalty in relationships. But often we don't know how to communicate or we project what the consequences might be of sharing our feelings. CUT-THRU broadens awareness to give you the security and courage to communicate, from the heart. It's this type of sincere care that sustains or renews friendships despite challenges, separation, or time. A friend of mine described to me how she used CUT-THRU to clear up a difficult miscommunication.

"My best friend and I were very close and shared our deepest feelings with each other. One day my friend shared she was overloaded at work and having some trouble understanding certain decisions made by her boss. As she communicated, it was clear she felt I wasn't understanding her and I felt she wasn't understanding me. We hit a standstill and the conversation never got resolved. Then she started to avoid me. I didn't know what to do. I could feel she was blaming me for not caring. And I felt she just 'knew what she knew' and didn't want to hear my true feelings. This hurt me and I started to feel angry and resentful. I decided to use CUT-THRU to deal with my hurt and see what to do. I practiced and my heart kept saying to just love her and forgive her. It was hard because I felt she wasn't forgiving me. But I kept cutting-thru and realized I had to forgive myself as well. As I practiced, I saw new perspectives of myself, of her, and our relationship. Eventually we had a deep talk. I had grown through my practice and was able to share my insights. Our friendship was renewed at a whole new level of respect. CUT-THRU enabled me to gain a maturity I don't think I would have found without this tool."

Many people stay angry with a friend forever and never dissolve the challenges in the relationship. Indifference isn't a solution because it doesn't have sincere care. Indifference shuts down the heart. Cutting-thru anger or indifference helps heart feelings resonate again. Stay mad forever if you so choose, but realize it's you who pays the price when you're angry about a dispute. Remember what anger does to your body, plus the loss of friendship. Try CUT-THRU if you're angry with a relative or friend. Practice sincerely. Let all the overcare emotions and thoughts concerning the issue fade away. As your heart feels peaceful, ask for an understanding of how to forgive, release and let go, then follow your heart on what to do next. You'll know if you want to continue the friendship or whether it's best for you both to part ways. Either way, you will have cleared your feelings and can be at peace with what you decide.

Falling in Love

People meet and fall in love. Their hearts open wide and their spirits soar. Their perceptions of life shift, day-to-day events flow smoothly, and even problems resolve more easily. What happened? Science is showing that when we love and care, a coherence is created in the electrical energies surrounding the heart. This freedom from stress makes people feel as if they're walking on air. So magnetic is the topic of love, that a myriad of best-selling books are written and movies produced about the feelings and magic of romance.

As you first fall in love, the stirring hormones of love produce energetic care. The potion of love provides a natural high, but after a while the mind and solar plexus lock in on the object of our affections with attachment and expectations. Worries and insecurities surface, overcares stack, and the relationship becomes stressed. People tend to place their security, peace, and happiness in the hands of their romantic partner. When that person doesn't live up to their expectations, the novelty of the relationship wears off. The heart begins to close down. Overcare starts with attachment to our energy investment in the relationship. Thus, the romance becomes a roller coaster ride, with the head creating the emotional ups and downs, and true care from the heart fading away. Lasting security can only be found in our own hearts, not in the actions or responses of another person.

One of the first things to be aware of when you fall in love is the potential for sexual delusion. Passion from sexual novelty creates hormonal addictions and overcares that blind intuitive discrimination concerning relationship compatibility. It's hard to see past the big blue eyes — nothing else seems to matter. In the beginning you love everything about your new partner. Later you wonder, where did that feeling of romance go?

The following story is similar to millions of people's stories. John and Sue fell in love. John had been married before but it was Sue's first time in love. She never knew it would be that good. The sex was powerful and they shared their deepest hearts. It didn't matter to Sue that John had recently been laid off and was living on unemployment. She knew he'd find a job. They were both committed to the relationship and couldn't wait to bring up children in the love they felt for each other. A few months after they married, Sue became pregnant. It was definitely time to talk about John getting a job. But John didn't seem interested. Three months after the baby was born, John told Sue he was out job hunting but she found him at a friend's house with another woman. Sue was crushed. Sue and John could not reconcile their differences. She filed for divorce.

Once you add real life responsibilities to romance, the shortcomings of both partners manifest and the relationship becomes a fertile ground for overcare anxiety. Without tools to sustain heart perception and true care, the stresses of today's world overload relationships to the point where separation seems the only alternative. Too often, the sequence is romance, blindness, marriage, divorce, and a child caught right in the middle. What would married life be if we added the commitment to practice CUT-THRU to the marriage vows? "Until death do us part, we promise to remember to CUT-THRU and stay in our hearts forever." This might sound a bit outrageous to suggest, but I offer it as a sincere gesture of hope for the challenge of marriage.

A Broken Heart

A broken heart or broken marriage can feel like a broken world. As you feel a disappointment and the mind turns it over and over, you reinforce the hurt feelings and perceptions of betrayal each time. Trying to understand from the mind only digs you deeper and deeper into a hole. Practice CUT-THRU to find peace and then you can perceive how to move forward with your life. The higher heart can't be broken, only the mind can — with its dashed hopes and shattered mind-sets of what should have been. Self-pity, self-blame, and insecurities destroy the ego vanity structure and the heart feels devastated. Left unchecked, the stress will accumulate into depression.

Why is it the heart feels broken? As I described earlier, it's because love and care have turned to lower heart feelings colored by sentiment, attachment, expectations, and sympathy from the mind. The unmanaged head has taken our initial feeling of love or care and added overcare to it. As a result, our heart frequencies become incoherent and disordered. When love is colored by attachment, when compassion becomes sympathy, when care turns to overcare, these feelings become lower heart frequencies because there is still some heart in them but the head has overruled your initial higher heart feelings.

A broken heart is when your head keeps playing the same sad movie over and over, creating a tremendous emotionalism. Head thoughts trigger hurt, anger, or resentment in the solar plexus and you feel insecure. Then you react to that insecurity with more head thoughts which further amplify the negative feelings until you are in a state of emotionalism. Emotionalism is the over-indulgence in unbalanced emotions. If you're at the point of tears, you can still choose to use your heart intelligence to manage your emotions. You can let a few tears come — something sincerely hurt. But if you let your mind replay the hurt over and over, your emotions will blow the situation way out of proportion and into emotionalism.

Repression

Repression is not management. Repression shuts down both the feeling of hurt and the heart. You become numb. To release hurt and resentment, it is necessary to open the heart again to access the intuitive understanding needed to let go and move on. Otherwise the unresolved and repressed issues pop up again and again as you search for answers, sometimes every day or every night. When people finally release hurt, anger, and betrayal in their life, it is the heart that resolves it, usually bit by bit. The head does not have the power to do so alone. The key is to CUT-THRU frequently to activate a full heart perspective and gain the peace and understanding you need.

Transforming Grief

Extreme stressors that you no longer can do anything about, such as your spouse divorcing you, your child developing a serious illness, or a loved one dying, can understandably cause you to feel like a victim for a while. The grief of deep loss can be extremely hard to bear and requires compassionate care. The process of grieving is lengthened when people sincerely (and innocently) do not know how to feel or perceive differently. They are doing the best they can. While grief does take time to heal, it is up to the individual how long. Lengthy grieving imprisons you in an attitude of grief, destroys the immune system, and ages you prematurely. Yet, many people believe an extended cycle of grieving is beneficial. What they are really saying is that eventually the process will provide hopeful new heart perceptions and complete itself. Once people know how to go direct to their heart intelligence for new understanding, the cycle of grief can be shortened considerably.

In love relationships especially, if you find yourself with a broken heart, it's easy to blame your partner for being unfair. If you use the fair heart in Step 3 of CUT-THRU, you can come out of a break-up with the strength it takes to be your own person and the love that allows someone to go their own way. Realize that lasting security comes only from within you and that you have to develop it yourself. Take a broken heart to heart and use it to reconnect with life.

The world is abundant with things to do and people to meet and love. The head says he or she is the only one who can fulfill you because your heart opened so much with that person. But your heart will open that much again and more — if you live from the deeper heart now. Use CUT-THRU to take what you've learned and find the intuitive flow that can unfold your next adventure. From the head you might go looking for another relationship to bolster your security again. Go for your own security first. Keep current with your practice of the tool. With deep sincerity, give yourself the understanding and compassion that a break-up is very difficult but it can also be a springboard to your next level of fulfillment with new gifts to bring with you.

Marriage and Families

Learning how to find relationship compatibility with another person can be especially trying. Watching the news, it's clear that domestic life is responsible for many of today's problems. Behind closed doors a lot of people let out their stresses from the day. The ones we have chosen to love and stand beside frequently receive the raw end of the deal. More women, rich and poor alike, are injured by the men in their lives than by car accidents, muggings, or rape combined. The number one health problem for American women is now domestic violence with four million cases reported annually.[50] The number of child abuse victims has increased by over 40% in the last ten years and is still on the rise. The divorce rate remains over 50%, and each year over 1,000,000 children are newly affected. One third of these children will never see one of their parents again.

Once you have a familiarity zone with someone, watch out, as arguments can quickly turn into battles. It doesn't take many episodes to drain your caring or your partner's. Most marriages require sincere effort on the part of both partners to make them work. Even matches made in heaven have their challenges. As two people choose to keep on investing care and love in each other, their relationship will appreciate in value and a deeper compatibility will emerge. True compatibility develops from the heart, and not from personalities. Two people can be total opposites and live together in bliss, while two just alike can drive each other crazy. True heart care shows you the other person's essence and overrides any annoyances or irritants that can stack into a pile of overcares. Using CUT-THRU will keep you close enough to work out your differences in effective ways. Add the tool to your daily maintenance plan, and find the love and care that grow between you with each new level of understanding. A mature marriage is a valuable accomplishment.

Family Values

Core family values lie dormant within the heart when there's not enough true care in the home. Genuine care experienced within the small family unit provides each member with support and strength in everything they do. The warmth of a real home generates true care. It's like a central battery charger where each unit returns to recharge. The warmth of "home is where the heart is" can be felt wherever people are connected at the heart level. It can be in the office, the classroom, or even on the street corner. The practice of loving and caring for people at deeper and more sincere levels can awaken family values within our households and eventually unfold throughout the global family. To care for all people like a family with one big backyard is the real hope for planetary health.

Adult/Child Relationships

Parents frequently equate overcaring about their children with caring for them. This is a serious misconception. Worry never brings balanced solutions to problems. Many parents can't work, sleep, or eat because of worrying about their children. And children can't wait to get away from a worrying parent. Some parents finally tire of overcaring and stop caring.

If you're the adult faced with the kid you "just can't do anything with," first of all remember, you're not alone. That phrase applies to even more kids today than when I was a boy. Over 50% of parents polled in an *L.A. Times* survey feel their children are undisciplined and lack morals. They feel frustrated and guilty not knowing what to do with them.[51] It is a most difficult situation not to overcare about your teenager getting pregnant or locked up for drugs. However, if your care about your child is stress producing, it's overcare, and won't help you or the child. Stop and have a talk with yourself. Realize over-care isn't doing any good and blocks the flow of care and communication. It robs closeness from a parent-child relationship and blocks solutions that can lead to improved behavior. Use CUT-THRU to find out what balanced care would be in your situation. CUT-THRU each overcare to find heart intuition answers to child-rearing challenges. I wrote my last book, *A Parenting Manual: Heart Hope for the Family,* to provide parenting tools that work to release stress, increase care, and gain intuitive understanding of how children perceive life.[52] By developing intuitive heart perception of children, parents can stay a step ahead in guiding them.

True care is love in the active modality. Fill a home with true care and you'll be providing what a child really needs. Warmth, understanding, and compassion, along with a firm bottom-line, draw children to their parents and create opportunities for real communication to develop. By practicing CUT-THRU, you learn how to deal with your own feelings and your child's feelings, thereby nourishing the parent-child bond. Remember, it's coherent care that gives you access to wisdom or the intelligence of the heart. When sincerely caring for children, life will reward you with a deeper awareness of yourself. You'll see yourself grow along with them, take challenges on together, and be there for each other.

Nurturing starts as care reaches heightened sensitivity. To feel nurtured is to feel so loved that you know the love will always be there. It's a love that's not sustained by conditions. It doesn't require perfection, but loves you for who you are, mistakes and all. A nurturing love can represent a pillar of strength in a child's life, a beacon to come back to. Nurturing is not over-parenting but a high level of love and care directed by intuition for the child's best. Even the word "nurturing" *feels* warm and secure.

Children who are truly cared for have a better chance at developing self-security early in life's maturing process. Every generation has had tough challenges growing up. Yet with the world in its present state of confusion and stress overload, I do believe that today's children are faced with the toughest route yet. The financial status in most families requires that both parents work, resulting in a fast-paced home life with less time together. According to the Children's Defense Fund, nearly 20% of children in the U.S. haven't had even a ten-minute conversation with a parent in a month. In trying to be both mother and father, earn income, and take care of the household, single working parents often have the most difficulty finding quality time to spend with their children, It's estimated that 12.9 million children in the U.S. now live in single-parent homes, an increase of over 200% since 1970. Most juvenile crime is perpetuated by children from single-parent households.

However, regardless of whether a parent is married or single, children in a consciously caring environment will learn and grow. Give them uncaring surroundings and they'll regress. We can start to remedy this by adding care back into their lives at home and at school. I've seen deeply embittered children soften and become secure again through the consistent application of love and care by their new foster parents. Young people can change and families grow stronger more quickly than you might think if people have tools to stop the drain of overcare and increase the intelligence of true care — whatever their circumstances might be.

Relationships with Pets

Many people respond with open hearts to the simple affection and loyalty of an animal. People have pets for companionship, protection, to help with disabilities, for income, or for sport. Many prefer coming home from work or school to a friendly greeting instead of an empty house. Over fifty percent of Americans now own a cat or a dog. A study showed that most pet owners (68%) regard their pets as full family members, 30% said they are close friends, and 96% described the pet's role in the family as very important. Pets may not be for everyone, but for some, pets are easier to love than people and offer an unconditional love back. To have a loyal friend that loves you no matter what is for many the only source of love they can trust.

The experience of caring for an animal has been shown to improve morale and promote health in the elderly or those in nursing homes. Research supporting the health benefits of pets ranges from the facilitation of social interaction to the physiological benefits of the presence of animals on cardiovascular responses. University of Pennsylvania and Maryland researchers found that a year after hospitalization for heart disease, the mortality rate of patients with pets was roughly one third that of patients without pets.[53]

A pet might be expected to benefit health because it is a companion to care for, to keep one active, to cuddle, to watch and play with, to make one feel safe, and to stimulate exercise. Pets keep care an active part of millions of people's lives. They help youngsters learn how to care and be responsible. Studies show that children with pets have a higher degree of empathy.[54] Some cultures give children animals at a certain age to cultivate care and responsibility. Of course, in former eras, more people lived on farms where caring for animals was a natural part of life.

However, it's important to point out that it's not so much an animal's love that's the beneficial factor, but the sincere love and care that pets draw out of people. At the same time, pets can also become a source of overcare and stress. There are dogs and cats who create more frustration than solace in their owners' lives. Dogs who bark all the time are especially stressful for owners and neighbors. It's not really the pet but how you respond to the pet that determines the benefit or not.

In summary, all relationships benefit from true care without the overcare. Learning to develop true care for yourself first will increase the quality of your care in any relationship.

**Chapter
8**

Tips on Using Cᴜᴛ-Tʜʀᴜ

When you try anything new, there's always the hope that you will have an immediate benefit. There are also potential pitfalls to prepare for, such as overcaring that you won't do it right, that it won't work for you, that it's not as effective as it was said to be, etc. Let's cover some of these potential obstacles first.

Obstacle #1

It's too hard. I won't be able to do it right.

Cᴜᴛ-Tʜʀᴜ steps are actually quite simple. Each step is progressive and in many situations Step 1 is all you'll need to find release. "Rain or Sunshine?" becomes an easy reminder that you can choose a broader and more hopeful perspective at any time. If you don't feel an uplifting understanding, go on to Step 2. Each step will take you to a new level of perception. Remember, it's *perception* that causes the rain, not the situation itself. People bump into their perceptions and react, assuming they see the whole picture. For deeper overcares, you will need to spend a little time re-tracing your perceptions in Step 4. But think of the time you've already spent and spent and spent going in circles on these issues. All the frustration, all the worry, all the anxiety, all the fear, all the energy drain! A little sincere heart application to go through each step is efficient use of energy that will CUT-THRU any obstacle in life and give you new direction. It's worth the care to learn these simple steps. The free energy released will inspire you to use this tool on any problem. Once you get a feel for how it works, it's an easy flow.

Obstacle #2

It won't work for me. My problems are much too big.

Whether a concern has been serious or long standing, such as severe anxiety, depression, death, abuse, job loss, addiction, etc., this tool has still been proven to work. Some people cope with multiple problems at once — fear of downsizing at work, a spouse's job stress, a personal health problem, abuse from the past, children who are troubled, an aging or ill parent, a sense of hopelessness that things aren't going to get any better, and more. This is not to say that relief won't require practice of the tool.

Long-standing problems took time and energy to construct and therefore will take a little time and energy to completely release from your cellular memory. But that's exactly what CUT-THRU is designed to do. Some people have been in therapy for years, then found CUT-THRU finally provided their breakthrough. One woman explained to me that as a child, when she was abused by her mother, she had to use her heart to survive. She would remember the fun times she had with her mom and that would remind her that her mom really did love her. She recognized CUT-THRU as a tool to do again what she did as a child, but now she could use all the steps and find a complete release. I'm not suggesting that people stop any form of therapy or any remedy that is helping them. I'm suggesting they add CUT-THRU to their efforts to care for themselves. If you don't try the tool, you'll never know what it might do for you.

Obstacle #3

I don't have time. I'm too busy.

True care is love in the active modality. Everyone seeks care and love — unless they've lost all hope that it's possible. People think that practicing tools is "too much trouble" or that "life is going so fast that if I add one more thing I won't be able to keep up." They have not been educated to understand that going deeper in the heart for direction releases the tyranny of time. For one moment, honestly assess the amount of time you now spend on overcare worry, anxiety, or insecurity. Now consider how much time you would save if you eliminated all that. Common sense would advise you that *you don't have time to not CUT-THRU.* I've talked to people who are so habituated to mentally and emotionally recycling their problems, they wonder what they'll do with all their time and extra energy after they CUT-THRU! Eliminating energy drains creates time shifts into more fun and quality living. It's the amount of heart you put into something that causes a time shift. People have the capacity to go deep in the heart and find the nectar of care and love, but first they have to learn to access it.

Obstacle #4

Other people can do this, but what if I fail?

Realize this tool is scientifically proven to work. You won't fail if you use it progressively. The fear of failure results from quitting or from not remembering to use the tool when you need it. People want regeneration, but it's the mind that keeps it from happening. Learning to perceive can be like walking through a hall of mirrors — a series of frames of perception — mind-distorted frames, or mind with some heart frames, or clear heart perception frames. Have patience with your mind as you learn to engage the heart more sincerely. As you keep practicing CUT-THRU, the coherent heart power generated will transmute the density and shrapnel of the mind, emotions, and cellular memories into breakthrough perspectives.

Don't look for perfection. Perfection is a ceiling that implies there's nowhere else to go and nothing new to perceive. Look for increasing ratios instead — increasing your ratio of insight versus confusion; increasing your ratio of listening to your heart versus your mind's insecurities; increasing your ratio of energy versus depletion. Have a sincere heart's desire to CUT-THRU. Then it's up to you to actualize what your heart perception provides you and ride the waves of life instead of getting caught in the undertows.

To accelerate heart intelligence, practice the tool while listening to the music *Speed of Balance*. This music was designed to facilitate perception shifts and emotional release from cellular memories. Practice the different steps as you relax to this musical adventure. As the scientific research in Chapter 5 shows, people experienced significant increases in feelings of caring, contentment, and vigor, and significant decreases in guilt, depression, and anxiety, along with an average 100% increase in the vitality hormone DHEA in thirty days when they practiced CUT-THRU while listening to *Speed of Balance*. Don't look for any particular experience in this holographic music. Just relax and listen from the heart.

Obstacle #5

But who will I be without my insecurity and overcare?

Many people become so used to overcare, insecurity, guilt, depression, etc., they build their identity around those feelings and attitudes. This blocks love and fulfillment. CUT-THRU does not strip away identity. It allows you to build new security based on insight and creative care, unfolding a *truer sense of who you really are*. At first there can be a feeling of emptiness as overcare leaves your system with all its old programs of "shoulds and should nots." If you feel empty, go deeper in the heart and feel compassion for yourself. Then find something to appreciate. A key part of CUT-THRU is not to just empty out, but to activate the higher heart feelings of love, care, compassion, and appreciation that are really there in the core of your heart. Once overcare is out of the way, the real you can emerge, overcare being the veil that separates you from your spirit or essence. You'll get in touch with your core power that has been there all along.

When you make a conscious effort to choose rain or sunshine, and then find one small thing to appreciate, you add energy to your system. One woman said that the first time she tried CUT-THRU she felt uncomfortable being at peace and overcared about that. As she continued through the steps, she started to feel higher heart feelings of compassion and appreciation fill the emptiness which gave way to a whole new feeling of empowerment. "I can do this, I can do this," she exclaimed excitedly. Freeing your spirit is something only you can do. The bottom-line is this — whatever insecurities, fears, habits, pitfalls, or objections might prevent you from using this tool— see if they, too, are not based in overcare or in not enough care for yourself.

Now let's discuss the new sense of hope and other enhancements you will discover as you use this tool.

Hope

Hope is a feeling that what is wanted is possible and that events will turn out well. Limited perception and doubt cut off the heart feeling of hope. Pessimism and hopelessness have been scientifically linked to premature aging and early death. And feelings of hopelessness just plain feel awful. Heart perception renews hope. With hope comes renewed energy and joy of life.

Realize that due to family upbringing and social programming, people slip into overcare and hopeless feelings innocently. You may be annoyed with your parents, your relatives, the educational system, the government, or society, but staying stuck in overcare or blame will drain your spirit and destroy hope. As you CUT-THRU, you find compassion and new hope for solutions.

Hope is an essential ingredient for managing perceptions and emotions in the Information Age. The mind can't possibly sort, comprehend, or utilize the flood of incoming data without the power of the heart. Understanding this will usher in the *real* Information Age — the Intuitive Age. CUT-THRU empowers both heart and mind to rejoice that you have the ability to choose intuitive perspectives and re-create your life. Once you experience the power you have to shift perception, you gain free energy and understanding that you can do it the next time. Use the tool whenever you catch yourself drawing against your energy account. *Remembering* to use the tool before life throws you a curve ball takes practice. It's an ongoing game you play with yourself until your heart muscle is strong enough to hold you in the flow of higher heart feelings and perceptions throughout the day and night.

To maximize your CUT-THRU practice, observe your energy expenditures throughout a day, and notice the overcares and insecurities. Use the tool to transform each one on the spot or during a break when you can complete the steps. CUT-THRU offers a door to the other side of human perception — a perceptual domain of intuitive intelligence where you co-create with life instead of being its victim. If you slip back or forget to use the tool and stack up a deficit, say to yourself, "Oops!" and immediately practice CUT-THRU again. Don't overcare or judge yourself for slipping back. Remember your root motive to begin with was right and have compassion for yourself. Just get back on your surfboard and ride the wave again. Remember it's not about perfection but about increasing ratios of success. Whatever obstacles you encounter, appreciate that you're building coherent power to CUT-THRU to a much easier flow in life.

Time Shifts

Feelings, thoughts, and perceptions are how people experience life. How we respond to that experience determines the outcome and quality of our relationship to time, people, and events. Emotional energy is actually neutral. Through our intent, we add emotional energy to thoughts and feelings. If you are enjoying a feeling of love, you often want to enhance it. For example, if you are caring for a toddler and enjoy a loving feeling with her, you may want to add energy to that experience. So you cuddle her to amplify the warm feeling. You value the time spent with her and time seems to fly. On the other hand, if the toddler splatters food on the floor and you feel irked cleaning it up, and then she spills the entire bowl all over you, you might add emotion to your irked feeling and explode in anger. You feel impatient and resent the time it takes to clean the floor and yourself. It seems to take forever. Your sense of time *shifts* according to the emotional quality of the time spent. It's your choice to add emotional energy to your experiences or not. It's your choice to CUT-THRU in the moment or not. You manage yourself *within a time span* — during the moment of overcare.

Another illustration of time shifts can be seen in how people approach traffic jams. If you yield to irritation in a traffic jam on the way to work, it's likely you'll carry that irritation to the office and feel irritable throughout the day. Then instead of going home to a welcome retreat, you're more vulnerable to being drained by the kids or irritated if supper isn't ready on time. When irritated, people often say things they later regret that will take them hours or days to clean up. If you CUT-THRU at the first irritation in the traffic jam, you divert all the negative outplay at the office and then at home. That's so much time and energy saved! One tool used to manage your emotions and align them with the heart at any time causes a *time shift* — it stops a chain link reaction of time and energy waste.

People often recognize they had a loss of time during periods when they didn't feel effective. As they use the tool and go back to the heart for direction, they'll see habitual energy drains fall by the wayside — and quietly know they could have gone the old way and lost a whole lot of time through being vulnerable to former patterns. By cutting-thru in the "now," you shift into a new time zone of effectiveness. It's never too late to pick up the tool. If you forget in the traffic jam, use CUT-THRU as soon as you remember. Don't think you've totally missed it. Cutting-thru at any moment creates a time shift that saves *stages* of time loss. Even if you forget to practice until you get home, use the tool at that point to normalize the situation at home. As you practice more, the tool will pop up in memory at earlier stages in the chain reaction. Each time you *actualize* an effort of practice, you create a time shift. As you stack up time shifts, you build a platform of basic peace in yourself. When more people can divert emotions that drain them and live in the "flow," it will be a giant step toward global peace.

When you build a quantity of mental and emotional time shifts, you can observe how that translates into the physical body. The physical body accumulates that much more energy for healing if you are unwell. Or it accumulates that much more energy to regenerate and feel buoyant if you are healthy. Making mental and emotional time shifts is especially important in preventing physical ailments or premature aging.

People often have insights about themselves and with good intentions decide to half-heartedly utilize their insights. They practice a little and maybe change a little. CUT-THRU is insight and do. Some know at times they could just do, but don't. With CUT-THRU, they can go deep in the heart and harness the power to do. It saves drain and time. It's a serious act of time management to manage the quality of time you spend doing anything. As you gain inner time management, then outer time issues will balance out.

Time Management

Standard formulas taught in time management courses help people become efficient, but they don't necessarily bring peace or *quality* time. Thousands have learned to exquisitely time manage their job, children, and household schedules, but if the mind and emotions aren't managed, they can still be very unhappy and unsatisfied. Time management can't be considered a time shift if it doesn't bring inner peace as well as outer convenience. You could call CUT-THRU higher octave time management because it deals with both the inner and the outer. It can manage your emotions and your to-do lists. The first adds to peace, happiness, and efficiency — the latter only adds to efficiency. CUT-THRU helps you activate the internal time manager which has the power to give you continuous time shifts. Time shifting catapults people into a new era of time management where there's much more fun and enrichment.

Remember that emotions can contribute tremendously to the fun in life or they can put you into total despair. Add emotions to balanced care, and the richness of that feeling will be amplified through your entire system. Time will seem to flow smoothly so everything gets done. Add emotions to overcare, and one unchecked worry can propagate more worries that drain and age you. Time then becomes a battle you fight against. A common-sense efficiency is to look after yourself so you can enjoy looking after your home, your job, and other people. The key is to recognize how emotions are affecting you. Then practice CUT-THRU to achieve total security and maximum energy.

Flex

Learning to flex from the heart builds flex-ability. Flex is love in a usable form. It rounds off the corners and edges of events in life. As you become flexible in your mental and emotional responses, you'll find less effort against resistances. CUT-THRU ignites your hope, but it's the power of your spirit that renews the joy of living. As spirit infuses your mental, emotional, and physical energies down to the cellular level, it unfolds a new blueprint for fulfillment in life.

Living from the heart is business — the business of caring for yourself. You become so efficient with your energy that you create a whole new momentum of adventure and fun. The world takes on a new dimension of perception that goes beyond time and space limitations. Check your inner weather throughout the day. If it's getting dry and irritable or rainy and sad, it's time to CUT-THRU. When there's just "too much to do," when life's "going too fast," when you feel like you're burdened, stop and CUT-THRU! Find the intuitive flow that will start to arrange your life more efficiently. Power up through loving yourself. Love disciplines the mind to stay tuned to the heart so you can perceive with true understanding. It becomes a game of how fast you can shift, then accelerate at the speed of balance.

Here are some commentaries on CUT-THRU from people who have been practicing the tool:

> "I'm a husband, father, and computer systems analyst. I've been in my head a lot of my life. Whenever I'm feeling uneasy, worried, or anxious about anything in particular, I love to use CUT-THRU. The thing I love most is that it really does what it says. It CUTS THROUGH the overcare and gets to the heart of the matter, the true care that I originally felt in my heart. I am able to get back to a very clear picture of what is the most efficient way to handle a potentially worrisome situation. I can easily turn overcare back into true care. In short, I can come to peace much more quickly with a lot of situations because CUT-THRU is a great tool for putting things into proper perspective."
>
> V.T., COMPUTER ANALYST, DALLAS, TX

> "I was facilitating a process recently for a group of CEOs. The process called for truthful, honest feedback. Midway through the process the tension began to mount as the executives shared insights that were difficult for some to hear. Harsh words were exchanged between several members of the group. As the facilitator, I realized that I could lose control of the group and the process if something were not done quickly to re-establish order. I could feel my own anxiety level rising,

accompanied by a sense of uncertainty as to how to meet this challenge. I used the CUT-THRU tool immediately. I had just learned it a few days earlier. My own balance and poise returned, along with a very creative idea for managing the situation. I was surprised by how quickly the solution came to me and by how quickly the executives responded to it. Order was almost instantly restored to the meeting which completely surprised (and delighted!) the group. I was later congratulated by the group on how I was able to resolve the conflict to the relief and satisfaction of all. I continue to be amazed by the efficiency and effectiveness of this tool."

J.K., EXECUTIVE CONSULTANT, SAN FRANCISCO, CA

"I am a Special Projects Manager for a large multinational corporation. My division began downsizing several months ago, along with drastic cost-cutting measures. Anxiety is at an all-time high and morale is at an all-time low. It had been very difficult for me to maintain my perspective and poise. Through consistently practicing CUT-THRU, I have been able to neutralize my anxiety almost completely which has astonished even myself. I find myself going through the workday with a sense of clarity and well-being, and I am able to make decisions with a much greater sense of self-confidence, which is being noticed and commented on by my co-workers. I am much less affected by the chaos and despondency shared by my colleagues. I am grateful to know about this tool."

T.S., SPECIAL PROJECTS MGR., SEATTLE, WA

"Since I started practicing CUT-THRU, absolutely amazing things have happened. First, as an ex-

ecutor of an estate, my personal assets were also frozen. This caused me much overcare. I practiced CUT-THRU and my heart directed me to talk to a different person at the bank who waived some of the rules and released enough money to pay my bills. Then I practiced CUT-THRU on my overcare about my body. In Step 4 I had to retrace my overcare back to an initial love for my body and accept a severe chronic health problem, Epstein Barr Syndrome, and accept my age (58). Two days later I had to show my I.D. at McDonald's because they did not believe I was eligible to receive the senior citizen discount. That's the first time that's happened to me. Friends are continuing to remark at how quickly my upsets are resolving and how calm and peaceful I seem to be. As an incest survivor, I have always avoided a relationship with a man. I had to work at the deepest levels of CUT-THRU to go back to the original point of love and care for myself before that traumatic childhood experience. I felt a release I had never before experienced. You know what happened a few days later? A wonderful man asked me for a date. The first one to ask in 39 years. I think I could CUT-THRU anything now. This tool is astounding."
D.C., PSYCHOLOGIST, PHOENIX, AZ

Creativity

Practicing CUT-THRU builds electrical coherence between the heart and brain. This causes rapid development of your higher faculties such as intuition, creativity, and especially clarity in decision-making processes. The higher the ratio of time that people use their higher faculties, the more their potential to enjoy life increases.

The heart is the door to creative intelligence.

Through emotional management from the heart, people tap into the highest form of creativity — re-creating their perceptions of reality. Creativity is an aspect of human intelligence that is not well understood, just as care is not well understood. Creativity is contact with your spirit, unveiling new perceptions and feelings of joy and excitement. Learn to differentiate between the inquiring mind versus the inquiring heart. Practice the tool to *consciously* understand yourself on many levels. Until you become more conscious, you'll remain a victim of habitual mental and emotional perceptions and reactions. As you CUT-THRU and put your heart intelligence first, you'll unfold your creative capacities for business, the arts, science, parenting, relationships, anything. Creativity quite simply starts with knowing how to be emotionally coherent and activating the power of your heart.

Much of the time when people visualize, daydream, or set goals, the creativity is mind-driven. That's why it doesn't always work. The world is living in a serious stress zone in desperate need of empowered creativity. The mind has been tried and tried. It's time for the heart. Opening your heart is a gift to yourself and the world. Whatever your obstacles are in life, it's better to wake up before it's too late. Use CUT-THRU to build a new planetary heart of care. Your heart intelligence will help you create cellular transformation, slow the aging process, and be truly creative in life. It can be a brand new world or it can keep on going in the same old merry-go-round. It's up to you. No one can do it for you, and you can't do it for anyone else. You can only care enough to give others your love and care and the tools they need to do it for themselves. My goal in this book has been to express my sincere care and provide a proven tool that people can use to find their own heart power and a shift to a new dimension of fulfillment in life.

References

1. Csikszentmihalyi, M., *Flow: The Psychology of Optimal Experience*. 1990, New York: Harper & Row.

2. Tiller, W., R. McCraty, and M. Atkinson, *Toward cardiac coherence; A new non-invasive measure of autonomic system order*. Alternative Therapies, 1996. In Press (Jan. Issue).

3. Neufeldt, V., ed. *Webster's New World Dictionary*. 3rd college ed. 1993, New York: Prentice Hall.

4. Research and Forecasts, I., *The Mitchum Report on Stress in the 90s*. 1990, New York: Revlon, Inc.

5. Montgomery, C.L., *The care-giving relationship: paradoxical and transcendent aspects*. Journal of Transpersonal Psychology, 1991. 23(2): pp. 91-103.

6. McCraty, R., *et al.*, *The effects of emotions on short term heart rate variability using power spectrum analysis*. American Journal of Cardiology, 1995. 76: pp. 1089-1093.

7. Damasio, A.R., *Descartes' Error*. 1994, New York: G P Putnam's Sons.

8. Henry, J.P., *Biological basis of the stress response*. Integr Physiol Behav Sci, 1992. 27(1): pp. 66-83.

9. Cowley, G., M. Hager, and A. Rogers, *Exhausted—Breaking Point*, in *Newsweek*. 1995 March 6; pp. 56-62.

10. Rubin, B.M., *Aging baby boomers becoming blind to ambition*, in *Chicago Tribune*. Jan 31, 1995.

11. Goleman, D., *EQ—Why your emotional intelligence quotient can matter more than IQ*, in *San Luis Obispo County Telegram-Tribune*. Sept. 8, 1995, pp. USA Weekend 4-6.

12. Goleman, D., *Emotional Intelligence: Why it can matter more than IQ*. 1995, New York: Bantam Books.

13. Ornstein, R. and D. Sobel, *The Healing Brain*. 1987, New York: Simon and Schuster.

14. Simone, D.d., *You're no Weak Sister, Sister*, in *Mademoiselle*. 1989 May; pp. 152-154.

15. Richardson, E., *The Age of Rage*, in *Elle*, 1995 May.

16. Kawachi, I., *et al.*, *Symptoms of anxiety and risk of coronary heart disease. The Normative Aging Study*. Circulation, 1994. 90(5): pp. 2225-9.

17. *Heart and Stroke Facts: 1995 Statistical Supplement*, American Heart Association.

18. Williams, R., *et al.*, *Type A behavior and elevated physiological and neuroendocrine responses to cognitive tasks.* Science, 1982. 218: pp. 483-485.

19. Rein, G. and R.M. McCraty, *Long term effects of compassion on salivary IgA.* Psychosomatic Medicine, 1994. 56(2): pp. 171-172.

20. Childre, D.L., *Speed of Balance: A Musical Adventure for Emotional and Mental Regeneration.* 1995, Planetary Productions: Boulder Creek.

21. Jemmott, J.B., *Social motives and susceptibility to disease.* Journal of Personality, 1987. 55: pp. 267-293.

22. Chopra, D., *Ageless Body, Timeless Mind.* 1993, New York: Harmony Books.

23. Cantin, M. and J. Genest, *The heart as an endocrine gland.* Clinical and Investigative Medicine, 1986. 9(4): pp. 319-327.

24. Pribram, K.H., *Brain and Perception: Holonomy and Structure in Figural Processing.* 1991, Hillsdale, NJ: Lawrence Erlbaum Associates, Publishers.

25. Kafatos, M. and R. Nadeau, *The Conscious Universe.* 1990, New York: Springer-Verlag.

26. Baggott, J., *The Meaning of Quantum Theory.* 1992, New York: Oxford University Press Inc.

27. Pearce, J.C., *Evolution's End.* 1992, New York: HarperCollins.

28. Stroink, G., *Principles of cardiomagnetism*, in *Advances in Biomagnetism*, S.J. Williamson, *et al.*, Editors. 1989, Plenum Press: New York, pp. 47-57.

29. McCraty, R., M. Atkinson, and W.A. Tiller, *New electrophysiological correlates associated with intentional heart focus.* Subtle Energies, 1995. 4(3): pp. 251-268.

30. Childre, D.L., *FREEZE FRAME®, Fast action stress relief.* 1994, Boulder Creek, CA: Planetary Publications.

31. Hafen, B., *et al.*, *The Health Effects of Attitudes Emotions and Relationships.* 1992, Provo: EMS Associates.

32. McClelland, D. and C. Kirshnit, *The effect of motivational arousal through films on salivary immunoglobulin A.* Psychology and Health, 1987. 2: pp. 31-52.

33. Rein, G., R.M. McCraty, and M. Atkinson, *Effects of positive and negative emotions on salivary IgA.* Journal for the Advancement of Medicine, 1995. 8(2): pp. 87-105.

34. Press, A., *Compound Being Tested Could Ease Aches of Aging*, in *San Jose Mercury News.* September 3, 1995.

35. Kerr, D.S., *et al.*, *Chronic stress-induced acceleration of electrophysiologic and morphometric biomarkers of hippocampal aging*. Society of Neuroscience, 1991. 11(5): pp. 1316-1317.

36. Press, A., *American Workers Feel Burned Out*, in *Los Angeles Times*. Sept. 3, 1993: LA. p. 2.

37. Skrzycki, C., *Healing the Wounds of Success*, in *The Washington Post*. July 23, 1989.

38. Spake, A., *Behavior Struggles in Stress City*, in *The Washington Post*. January 13, 1985, p. 4.

39. *Depression Taking a Toll in the Workplace*, in *San Jose Mercury News*. March 5, 1995,

40. Granberry, M., *Battling Burnout*, in *Los Angeles Times*. October 20, 1988.

41. Papadatou, D. and F. Anagnostopoulos, *Factors contributing to the development of burnout in oncology nursing*. British Journal of Medical Psychology, 1994. 67(2): pp. 187-199.

42. Smollar, D., *Teacher's Flight*, in *Los Angeles Times*. Sept. 30, 1991, p. 1.

43. Green, J. and R. Shellenberger, *The subtle energy of love*. Subtle Energies, 1993. 4(1): pp. 31-55.

44. Morris, A.F., *Justifiable Paranoia Afflicts Lawyers*, in *Los Angeles Times*. May 1, 1994, p. 27.

45. *Golf Stress is Killing the Japanese*, in *The Wall Street Journal*. June 16, 1993.

46. Oates, B., *Stress in Coaching*, in *Los Angeles Times*. July 13, 1989, p. 1.

47. Ludovise, B., *When Athletes Decide the Thrill is Gone*, in *Los Angeles Times*. May 2, 1990, p. C1.

48. Williams, R.B., *et al.*, *Prognostic importance of social and economic resources among medically treated patients with angiographically documented coronary artery disease*. Journal of the American Medical Association, 1992. 276: pp. 520-524.

49. Lynch, J., *The Broken Heart: The Medical Consequences of Loneliness*. 1977, New York: Basic Books.

50. Nahser, F.B. and S.E. Mehrtens, *What's Really Going On*. 1993, Frank C Nahser Inc.

51. *LA Times Poll*, in *Los Angeles Times*. June, 1991.

52. Childre, D.L., *A Parenting Manual: Heart Hope for the Family*. 1995, Boulder Creek: Planetary Publications.

53. Lohmeier, L., *The Healing Power of Pets*, in *East West*. 1988 June; pp. 51-53.

54. Poresky, R.H. and C. Hendrix, *Differential effects of pet presence and pet-bonding on young children*. Psychological Reports, 1990. 67(1): pp. 51-54..

INSTITUTE OF HEARTMATH Published Research Studies

G. Rein, R. McCraty. Long Term Effects of Compassion on Salivary IgA. *Psychosomatic Medicine*, 1994:56(2): 171-72, abst.

R. McCraty, M. Atkinson, W. A. Tiller, and G. Rein. New Electrophysiological Correlates Associated With Intentional Heart Focus. *Subtle Energies*, 1995:4(3): 251-262.

D. Rozman, R. Whitaker, T. Beckman, and D. Jones. Initial Use of a New Intervention Program for Significantly Reducing Psychological Symptomatology in HIV-Seropositive Individuals. *Psychosomatics*, 1995:36(2): 207, abst.

R. McCraty, M. Atkinson, W. A. Tiller, and G. Rein. Autonomic Assessment Using Power Spectral Analysis of Heart Rate Variability in Emotional States. *Psychosomatic Medicine*, 1995:57(1): 84-85, abst.

G. Rein, R. McCraty, M. Atkinson. The Physiological and Psychological Effects of Compassion and Anger. *Journal of Advancement in Medicine*, Summer 1995:8(2): 87-105.

Scientific Papers in Press

R. McCraty, M. Atkinson, W. A. Tiller, G. Rein, and A. Watkins. The Effects of Emotions on Short Term Heart Rate Variability Using Power Spectrum Analysis. *American Journal of Cardiology*, 1995:76(14):1089-1093.

R. McCraty, W. A. Tiller, M. Atkinson. Towards Cardiac Coherence: A New Non-Invasive Measure of Autonomic System Order. *Alternative Therapies in Health and Medicine*, Jan. 1996.

Funding

IHM research is supported by private donations, as well as foundations and corporations. IHM is a 501(c)(3) nonprofit corporation; donations are tax-deductible. All donations are gratefully received to make it possible for us to continue these research efforts.

INSTITUTE OF HEARTMATH INDIVIDUAL RETREAT PROGRAMS

IHM's retreat programs are full, in-depth learning adventures blending classroom instruction, personal and interactive exercises, and private time for reflection. Located amidst the splendor of the Northern California Redwoods, you'll enjoy the beauty of nature and the rejuvenation of this tranquil setting.

Heart Empowerment Retreat I & II

Gives you a transforming experience and simple tools to begin a life of greater vitality, more creativity and more love. Based on the book *Hidden Power of the Heart*, by Sara Paddison. Heart Empowerment II teaches advanced HeartMath tools and applications.

"Powerful, excellent, profound and empowering information backed up by evidence that it works."
Beatrice Culver, Executive Board, Center for International Dialogue

The Inner Quality Management Retreats and Seminars

This program facilitates an in-depth experience to help you dramatically reduce your stress, cut through work challenges efficiently and learn how to revitalize yourself as you go.

"The techniques of HeartMath . . . have proved to be a turning point in our corporate development and culture. HeartMath added a new dimension to our approach to business problems and I would recommend it to professionals dealing with the complex issues of teamwork."
Scott M. Burkhart, Director, Cardiovascular Business, Instromedix

Women's Empowerment Retreat

Designed for the woman of today who is challenged by the growing demands of family, relationships and career. It's a chance to get back in touch with your own personal goals, dreams and desires.

"It will change your life and those around you . . ."
Brenda Carlin, Producer/Self-Retired, Carlin Productions

The Empowered Parent Retreat

Offers hope for both parents, child care providers and teachers, presenting refreshing insights and powerful tools for raising children in today's world.

Based on the book *A Parenting Manual: Heart Hope for the Family*, by Doc Lew Childre.

"Being a single, working mother of a teenage boy, I learned tools in this seminar that brought balance and harmony to our hectic life..."
Robin Jordon, Ben Lomond, CA

FOR MORE INFORMATION ON HEARTMATH RETREATS
CALL 1-800-450-9111

Cut-Thru Workshops

Cut-Thru workshops provide hands-on instruction and practical applications of the Cut-Thru technique. These powerful and practical half-day programs are available on-site for corporations, governmental agencies and public institutions through certified HeartMath trainers and at IHM's research facility. Call 1-800-450-9111 for more information.

Cut-Thru Audiobook

This simple technique which eliminates the "burn-out" syndrome is now available as an audiobook. You'll be surprised at how easy it is to "Cut-Thru" long-standing emotional issues and even what seem to be "unsolvable" situations, just by practicing this proven technique. A valuable investment for anyone who wants to be in control of their mental, emotional and physical well-being.

Item #3120 $16.95

Cut-Thru Asset/Deficit Worksheets

A convenient easy-to-use form for practicing the Cut-Thru technique. Helps you define issues, conflicts and events that are draining your energy and determine how to Cut-Thru to new levels of insights and solutions. Transform deficits into assets.

Item #1024 $6.95

Freeze-Frame® Products & Programs

The Freeze-Frame technique is a core tool in the HeartMath system. It provides a foundation which all the training programs and retreats are built.

Freeze-Frame Workshops

Freeze-Frame workshops provide hands-on instruction and practical applications of the Freeze-Frame technique. These powerful and practical half-day programs are available on-site for corporations, governmental agencies and public institutions through certified HeartMath® trainers and at IHM's research facility. Call for more information.

Freeze-Frame Research/Training Video

This powerful training video features an in-depth presentation of the leading-edge scientific research behind Freeze-Frame, along with step-by-step instruction and personal interviews from professionals illustrating the impact and diverse applications of this innovative, self-management technique. Used alone or as part of meetings, special programs or training sessions, this high-quality tool is an excellent resource for trainers, consultants and organizations in need of stress management, team building, improved customer service, organizational development, enhanced communication skills and project planning. *Item #4010 $595.00 plus shipping and handling (Item #4012 $40.00 preview fee), lease/purchase agreements available*

FREEZE-FRAME Worksheets

A convenient, easy-to-use form for written FREEZE-FRAME exercises. Encourages faster development of FREEZE-FRAME skill.

Item #1045 $6.95 (pad of 50 worksheets)

FREEZE-FRAME: Fast Action Stress Relief
A Scientifically Proven Technique

By Doc Lew Childre

This best seller from the HeartMath series offers a proven technique for managing stress, improving communication skills and increasing your personal effectiveness. It's hard to believe something so easy can make such a difference in your life — but it can!

"If you're upset, the heart feels it. What you can do in the moment to calm yourself down is called Freeze-Frame."

Dr. Donna Willis, NBC News' *"Today Show"*

Item #1040 *$9.95*

FREEZE-FRAME Audiobook

The FREEZE-FRAME Audiobook, which includes musical compositions from Doc Lew Childre's latest "Designer Music" release, is invaluable to anyone who prefers listening to reading. Includes step-by step instruction of the FREEZE-FRAME technique by Bruce Cryer, one of the nation's leading business consultants.

". . . a research based system for taking charge of our own well-being and peace of mind."

The Voice (Richmond, VA)

Item #3145 $16.95

FREEZE-FRAME Inner Fitness System

The FREEZE-FRAME Inner Fitness System provides you with everything you need to start your own "Inner Fitness" program. Develop the mental and emotional "muscles" you need to renew your zest for life, boost your energy level and achieve maximum potential. This special offer includes:

- *FREEZE-FRAME* video and book
- *Heart Zones* (designer music)
- FREEZE-FRAME Worksheets
  an $83.00 value

With cassette	Item #1043	$59.95
With CD	Item #1044	$64.95

More Books and Music from Planetary

A Parenting Manual
Heart Hope for the Family
By Doc Lew Childre

Parenting in the '90s requires new insights, broader understanding and practical solutions. *A Parenting Manual* offers new perspectives for today's parents. Shows you how to give yourself the care and support you need to parent effectively, provide a firm, family foundation based on love and understand important stages in your child's development.

Item #1095 $14.95

Teaching Children to Love
55 Games and Fun Activities for
Raising Balanced Children in Unbalanced Times

By Doc Lew Childre

Teaching Children To Love offers parents, teachers and child care providers a complete hands-on guide for having fun while developing positive, healthy, life skills in children of all ages. Presented in a step-by-step format for family, classroom and youth program settings. Based on the tools and techniques presented in *A Parenting Manual.*

Item #1145 $14.95

The How to Book of Teen Self Discovery
Helping Teens Find Balance, Security & Esteem
By Doc Lew Childre

Find help, hope and solutions in this book written specifically for teens. Approved as a textbook in the state of California, *Teen Self Discovery* offers easy tools for developing inner-security and communication and listening skills, while managing emotions and reactions. Teens learn how to make positive choices and successfully meet the challenges of today's world.

Item #1065 $8.95

Self Empowerment:
The Heart Approach to Stress Management
By Doc Lew Childre

A comprehensive view of today's social issues and how each individual can make a positive difference. An essential book for understanding that making changes within yourself is the first step toward world change.

"*The message is a strong one and the methodology can be understood by many. The potential release of positive energy is formidable.*"

J. Tracy O'Rourke, Chairman and CEO, Varian Associates, Inc.

Item #1120 $13.95

The Hidden Power of the Heart
Achieving Balance and Fulfillment In A Stressful World

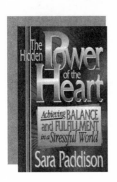

By Sara Paddison

A warm and fascinating account of a journey through the heart to find more love and happiness. Told with a simple yet profound understanding of spirituality, our holographic universe and the role of the heart in claiming our "intuitive intelligence."

"*Sara Paddison's book will revitalize the truth whereby one can not only consult one's heart but can actually listen to what it says. This book should be required reading.*"

Dr. Vernon H. Mark, Director Emeritus, Boston City Hospital

Item #1060 $11.95

Heart Zones

By Doc Lew Childre

Based on advanced research on the physical and emotional effects of music on the listener, *Heart Zones* is an intelligent blending of creativity and science. This four song musical composition designed to boost vitality and facilitate mental and emotional balance is the first music of its kind—'Designer Music'—to reach the *Billboard* charts where it remained for a year.

Cassette	Item #3170	$9.95
CD	Item #3175	$15.95

"Like a psychological cup of coffee without the side effects."
USA Today

Speed of Balance
A Musical Adventure for
Emotional & Mental Regeneration

By Doc Lew Childre

Doc Lew Childre's follow-up to his landmark release *Heart Zones*. *Speed of Balance** features eight new songs that have been arranged to create a cascading effect that leaves the listener with more energy and feeling ready to move on with life. Jazz enthusiasts, classical lovers and even rock-n-rollers find it revitalizing and entertaining. *Speed of Balance* represents the next step in music scientifically designed to make you feel good as well as entertain.

Cassette	Item #3250	$9.95
CD	Item #3255	$15.95

*A recent study showed that people can raise their own levels of the anti-aging hormone DHEA by practicing the new CUT-THRU technique and listening to *Speed of Balance*.

Ordering Information

For convenience, place your order using our toll-free number — 1-800-372-3100, 24 hours a day, 7 days a week or fax us your order at 408-338-9861. To order books, videos, tapes and compact discs, please send check, money order or credit card information to:

Planetary Publications
P.O. Box 66, Dept. RBK
Boulder Creek, California, 95006
800-372-3100/408-338-2161/Fax 408-338-9861
hrtmath@netcom.com
http://www.webcom.com/hrtmath

♦ Please include shipping and handling cost:
$5.25 for first item,
$1.00 each additional item.

♦ Foreign Orders:
Please call for accurate shipping rates.

♦ California residents include 7.25% sales tax.

♦ Santa Cruz County residents include 8.25% sales tax.

♦ Visa, Mastercard, Discover Card, and American Express accepted. Please include expiration date, card number, full name on card, and signature.

About the Editors:

Deborah Rozman, Ph.D., Editor

Deborah Rozman is a psychologist, author, and Executive Director of the Institute of HeartMath. As Executive Director, she oversees IHM operations and is instrumental in developing training programs (based on IHM research) that teach people how to use the heart as a central source of intelligence within the human system. She certifies trainers in IHM programs on intuitional development and creativity, women's empowerment, parenting, and personal effectiveness. She has edited dozens of books on the psychology of human development and authored five of her own. Deborah studied attitude change theory and psychology at the University of Chicago and has spent the past twenty years researching the psychology of consciousness. Prior to joining IHM, she was executive vice president of Biogenics, Inc. and directed their research programs with Harvard University. Deborah is a frequent keynote speaker and spokesperson for IHM.

Rollin McCraty, Contributing Editor

Rollin McCraty is Director of Research for the Institute of HeartMath, where he directs all scientific and clinical research projects. Rollin has co-authored numerous scientific papers on the electrophysiology of the human system and has presented these findings at dozens of medical and scientific conferences throughout the world. Before joining the IHM staff, Rollin was co-founder and senior engineer of Static Control Services, specializing in electrostatic consulting to a long list of corporations such as Hughes, IBM, Texas Instruments, Sony and Litton. He pioneered state-of-the-art technology in manufacturing and his inventions and product designs have become industry standards. He is published in engineering journals, magazines and reference books, and served on the IEEE Standards Committee. Rollin is also a frequent keynote speaker and spokesperson for IHM research.

Sara Hatch Paddison, Contributing Editor

Sara Paddison is Vice President of IHM and has worked extensively with Doc Lew Childre over many years in developing the HeartMath® system. Sara is the author of two books and editor of many more. Her popular book, *The Hidden Power of the Heart*, is the basis of IHM's successful Heart Empowerment® seminars. As editor of Doc Lew Childre's book, *A Parenting Manual: Heart Hope for the Family*, Sara is especially concerned with helping parents and families transform their stresses and find more balance and fulfillment in life. She is now editing Doc's next book, *Teaching Children to Love: 55 Games and Fun Activities for Raising Balanced Children in Unbalanced Times*. This book shows parents, educators and counselors how to teach CUT-THRU and other HeartMath self-management tools to children.

About the Author:

Doc Lew Childre is founder, president and CEO of the Institute of HeartMath, a nonprofit research and training organization in Boulder Creek, California. Incorporated in 1991, IHM is dedicated to providing practical stress solutions and well-tested approaches to quality, creativity and intuitive development. In developing the HeartMath® system for personal and organizational effectiveness, Doc spent twenty years researching the role of the brain, mind and heart in the human system. He is a consultant to Fortune 500 companies on Intui-Technology®, a program he designed to create quantum time shifts in decision-making and productivity. IHM training programs are frequently presented to corporations, health and governmental organizations, all four branches of the armed services, and educational associations. Dozens of corporate and educational trainers have been certified by IHM to conduct HeartMath trainings.

Doc's innovative technologies for mental/emotional self-management and empowerment have been featured on *NBC News'* "*Today Show,*" in *USA Today*, and in hundreds of other publications. Doc is also a music researcher whose albums *Heart Zones* and *Speed of Balance* were designed to create specific beneficial effects on human physiology and enhance mental and emotional balance in the listener. Doc is the author of five books, including the popular *FREEZE-FRAME®: Fast Action Stress Relief,* which is used by individuals and companies throughout the world for stress intervention and unleashing creativity.

CUT-THRU® READY- REFERENCE STEPS

Step 1. Recognize feelings and thoughts of overcare — Take an inner weather report. See if your inner weather is rain or sunshine. Then change your weather to prevent a flood. Choose the more hopeful perspective.

Step 2. Hold overcare thoughts or feelings in the heart. Remember, adapting stops the energy drain. Pretend you are floating on a raft or soaking in a heart-warming bath for a few moments. If the disturbed feelings won't release, or if your emotions are really revved up, homogenizing or blending the feelings in the heart helps the energy disperse so you can see a new perspective.

Step 3. Find your peace. As the current of discomfort dissipates, a new sense of peace and intuitive knowing can emerge. Hold to any feeling of peace. Then go to the "fair heart" to see and reflect clearly.

Step 4. Find the reference point of care. Ask yourself, "Why did I originally care?" Recall those beginning feelings of care for a few moments. Then ask yourself, "How did my original care slowly leak away due to overcare and drain me?" Recognize how your care was taken to inefficient extremes. Recall the original care and find the higher heart perspective.

Step 5. Follow your heart intelligence. In this last step, with clear perception and feelings of security coming back, listen to your heart to know what *true care* would now be in this situation. Follow your true care. That's caring for self and others

Top-Detach and save for your personal reference

Bottom-Detach & Mail for more information

CUT-THRU® READY- REFERENCE - KEY TERMS

Step 1 - Check your inner weather — "Rain or Sunshine?"

Step 2 - Adapt to stop the energy drain. "Float, soak, or blend" feelings in the heart.

Step 3 - Find "Fair Heart."

Step 4 - Recall "Original Care" or go to deeper neutral to save energy until you can find a "Higher Heart Feeling."

Step 5 - "Follow your Heart Intelligence" — Using Heart Intelligence connects you with intuitive insight and rebuilds mental and emotional energy reservoirs.

CUT-THRU® is a registered trademark of the INSTITUTE OF HEARTMATH. For more information call (408) 338-8700 or write IHM P.O. Box 1463, Boulder Creek, CA 95006

PLACE
STAMP
HERE

Planetary Publications
P.O. Box 66-CUT
Boulder Creek, CA 95006